Management Accounting (MA)
Diploma in accounting and business
Pocket Notes

British library cataloguing-in-publication data

A catalogue record for this book is available from the British Library.

Published by:
Kaplan Publishing UK
Unit 2 The Business Centre
Molly Millars Lane
Wokingham
Berkshire
RG41 2QZ

ISBN 978-1-83996-410-7

© Kaplan Financial Limited, 2023

Printed and bound in Great Britain.

Contents

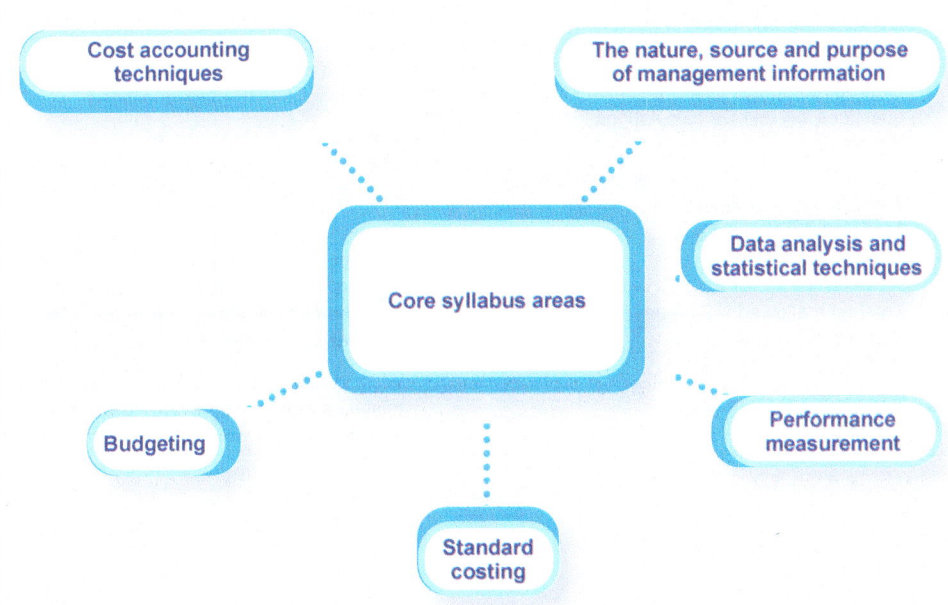

Exam guidance – keys to success in this paper

The syllabus is assessed by a two-hour paper or computer-based examination. Some questions will involve calculations, others will not.

	Number of marks
Thirty five 2-mark questions	70
Three 10-mark questions	30
Total marks	100

Total time allowed – 2 hours
Pass mark – 50%

Divide the time you spend on questions roughly in proportion to the marks allowed. Spend approximately 84 minutes on the 2-mark questions, leaving approximately 36 minutes for the 10-mark questions.

The exam is designed to test your understanding of principles, not just whether you can regurgitate information.

Read the question carefully and work through any calculations. Watch for words like "not" – for example some questions ask whether something is true and others whether it is not true.

Work steadily. Rushing leads to careless mistakes and questions are designed to include answers which results from careless mistakes.

Computer-based exam tips

Make sure you understand the software before you start. If in doubt ask the assessment centre staff to explain it. You can try a CBE Demo if you visit the Exam Support section of the ACCA's website.

Don't panic if you realise you have answered a question incorrectly. Getting one question wrong will not mean the difference between passing and failing.

You will receive your results immediately at the end of the exam.

You can take a CBE at any time in the year – you do not have to wait until the June or December exam sitting.

Linear regression

$$r = \frac{n \sum xy - \sum x \sum y}{\sqrt{[n \sum x^2 - (\sum x)^2][n \sum y^2 - (\sum y)^2]}}$$

If $y = a + bx$,

$$b = \frac{n \sum xy - \sum x \sum y}{n \sum x^2 - (\sum x)^2} \quad \text{and} \quad a = \frac{\sum y}{n} - b\frac{\sum x}{n}$$

Economic order quantity

$$\text{Economic order quantity} = \sqrt{\frac{2C_0 D}{C_H}}$$

$$\text{Economic batch quantity} = \sqrt{\frac{2C_0 D}{C_H\left(1 - \frac{D}{R}\right)}}$$

Arithmic mean

$$\bar{x} = \frac{\sum x}{n} \qquad \bar{x} = \frac{\sum fx}{\sum f} \quad \text{(frequency distribution)}$$

Standard deviation

$$\sigma = \sqrt{\frac{\sum(x - \bar{x})^2}{n}} \qquad \sigma = \sqrt{\frac{\sum fx^2}{\sum f} - \left(\frac{\sum fx}{\sum f}\right)^2}$$

(frequency distribution)

Variance $= \sigma^2$

Co-efficient of variation $\quad CV = \dfrac{\sigma}{\bar{x}}$

Expected value $\quad EV = \sum px$

Quality and accuracy are of the utmost importance to us so if you spot an error in any of our products, please send an email to mykaplanreporting@kaplan.com with full details, or follow the link to the feedback form in MyKaplan.

Our Quality Co-ordinator will work with our technical team to verify the error and take action to ensure it is corrected in future editions.

Accounting for Management

In this chapter

- Management, Cost and Financial accounting.
- Data and information.
- Mission statement.
- Planning, decision making and control.
- Levels of planning.

It is important that you understand the information needs of managers, and in particular the different types of responsibility centres.

Management, Cost and Financial accounting

- Financial accounting: recording financial transactions and summarising them in periodic statements for external users.

- Cost accounting: recording data and producing information about the costs of products, activities and responsibility centres.

- Management accounting: provision of information about historical and future costs of products and services, providing financial and non-financial information to managers.

	Management accounting	Financial accounting
Information mainly produced for	Internal use: e.g. managers and employees	External use: e.g. shareholders, payables, lenders, banks, government
Purpose of information	To aid planning, control and decision making	To record the financial performance in a period and the financial position at the end of that period
Legal requirements	None	Limited companies must produce financial accounts
Formats	Management decide on the information they require and the most useful way of presenting it	Limited companies must produce financial accounts

	Management accounting	Financial accounting
Nature of information	Financial and non-financial	Mostly financial
Time period	Historical and forward-looking	Mainly an historical record

Data and information

Data and information are different.

- Data consists of numbers, letters, symbols, raw facts, events and transactions which have been recorded but not yet processed into a form suitable for use.

- Information is data which has been processed in such a way that it is meaningful to the person who receives it (for making decisions).

Attributes of good information:

The 'ACCURATE' acronym:

- A – Accurate
- C – Complete
- C – Cost-effective
- U – Understandable
- R – Relevant
- A – Authoritative
- T – Timely
- E – Easy-to-use!

Mission statement

The mission statement is a statement in writing that describes the overall aims of an organisation.

There are four main elements:

- Purpose
- Strategy
- Policies and culture
- Values

Planning, decision making and control

The main functions of management are planning, decision making and control.

The process	What is it?	Information needs
Planning	• First part of the decision making process • Establishing objectives and formulating strategies to achieve objectives short-term (tactical) or long-term	• What has happened in the past • What might happen in the future
Decision making	• Considering information provided and making an informed decision • Choosing between alternatives	• Reliable information on different courses of action • The consequences of different options
Control	• The second part of the decision making process • Comparing information on actual and planned results to take control measures and amend plans	• Information on actual results • Plans or targets • Internally-produced feedback

Levels of planning

Strategic, tactical and operational planning

Information systems at different business levels

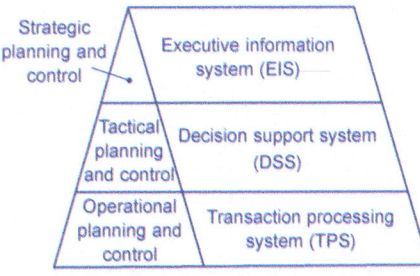

2

Cost classification

In this chapter

- Responsibility centres.
- Classifying costs.
- Element.
- Function.
- Nature.
- Behaviour.
- The high-low method – analysing costs into fixed and variable elements.
- Cost equations.
- Cost codes.

It is vital that you understand the different ways of classifying and describing costs, and when a particular perspective is appropriate.

You also need to be aware of the high-low method as a way of splitting semi-variable costs into their fixed and variable components and the use of cost equations to estimate future costs.

Responsibility centres

A responsibility centre is an individual part of a business whose manager has personal responsibility for its performance. The main responsibility centres are:

- cost centre
- profit centre
- investment centre
- revenue centre.

Managers must be able to plan and control the areas of performance on which they are measured.

	Cost centre	Profit centre	Investment centre	Revenue centre
What is it?	Part of the business for which costs are identified and recorded	Part of the business for which costs incurred and revenue earned are identified and recorded	A part of the business for which profits and capital employed are measured	A part of the business for which revenues earned are identified and recorded
Where might it be found?	Any production or service location, function, activity, item of equipment	Divisions of large organisations. May include several cost and revenue centres	Business units of large organisations	Sales divisions
How is performance measured?	Have cost targets been achieved?	What profit has been made by the centre?	Return on capital employed	What revenue has been earned?
What are the manager's information needs?	Costs incurred and charged to cost centre	Information about costs and revenues allocated to the profit centre	Information on costs, revenues and capital employed by the investment centre	Sales revenue earned by the individual revenue centre

	Cost centre	Profit centre	Investment centre	Revenue centre
Example	Audit, tax, accountancy departments in an accounting firm	Wholesale and retail divisions in a paint company	UK and European divisions of a multinational company	Regional sales areas within the retail division of a manufacturing company

Definition

A **cost object** is any activity for which a separate measurement of cost is undertaken e.g. a product.

A **cost unit** is a unit of product or service in relation to which costs are ascertained e.g. a hotel room.

A **cost centre** is a production or service location, function, activity or item of equipment for which costs can be ascertained e.g. a ward in a hospital.

Cost cards

The **cost card** for a cost object, unit or centre brings together all the costs relating to it.

Example – cost card for a product

	$
Direct materials	X
Direct labour	X
Direct expenses	X
PRIME COST	**XX**
Variable production overheads	X
VARIABLE COST OF PRODUCTION	**XX**
Fixed production overheads	X
TOTAL PRODUCTION COST	**XX**
Non-production overheads	X
TOTAL COST OF A UNIT	**XXX**

Classifying costs

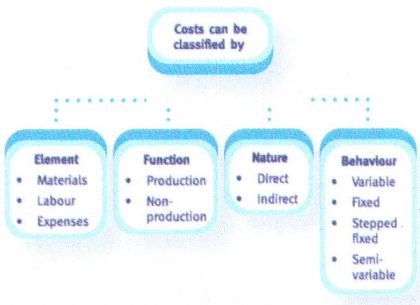

Element

Materials – all costs of materials purchased for production and non-production activities.

Labour – all staff costs relating to employees on the payroll of the organisation.

Expenses – all other costs which are not material or labour.

Function

Definition

Production costs are those incurred when raw materials are converted into finished and part-finished goods.

Non-production costs are costs not directly associated with the production processes in a manufacturing organisation.

Production costs

Direct materials

Materials which go into making the product

Direct labour

Labour directly involved in making the product

Direct expenses

Cost of expenses directly involved in making the product

Variable production overheads

Indirect costs that relate to production that vary in direct proportion to the quantity manufactured

Fixed production overheads

Indirect costs that relate to production that do not alter if the quantity manufactured changes

Non-production costs

Administrative costs
Costs of running general admin

Selling costs
Costs associated with marketing and taking orders

Distribution costs
Costs of distributing finished products

Finance costs
Costs incurred in financing an organisation

Nature

Definition

Direct costs

- Costs which can be directly identified with a specific unit or cost centre

- Total of direct costs = direct materials + direct labour + direct expenses = prime cost

Indirect costs

- Costs which cannot be directly identified to a specific unit or cost centre

- Indirect costs = indirect materials + indirect labour + indirect expenses = overheads

Behaviour

Cost behaviour is:

- the way in which input costs vary with different levels of activity

- understanding of cost behaviour central to budgeting, costing and decision making.

Variable cost

Definition

A cost that varies with the level of activity e.g. direct materials cost

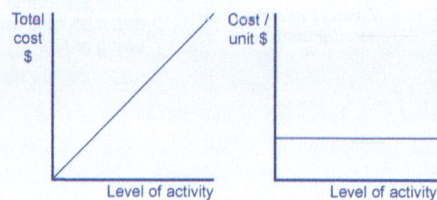

Fixed cost

Definition

A cost that is incurred for a period and that, within certain output and sales revenue limits, is unaffected by changes in the level of activity (output or sales revenue) e.g. factory rent.

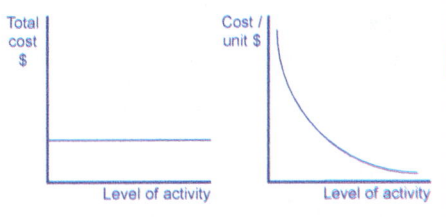

Stepped fixed cost

Definition

A fixed cost which is only fixed within certain levels of activity. Once the upper activity level is reached a new level of fixed cost becomes relevant e.g. warehouse costs and supervisors' wages.

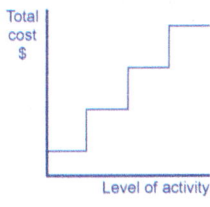

Semi-variable cost

Definition

Cost with a fixed and variable element e.g. telephone charges with fixed rental and charge per call.

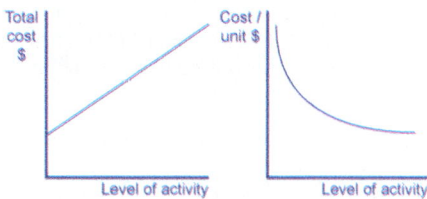

The high-low method – analysing costs into fixed and variable elements

Step 1: select high and low activity levels and their associated costs

Step 2: find variable cost per unit

Step 3: find fixed cost by substitution

$$\text{Variable cost per unit} = \frac{\text{Change in cost}}{\text{Change in level of activity}}$$

Fixed cost = Total cost – total variable cost

- High-low method can still be used with care if there are stepped fixed costs or changes in the variable cost per unit.

Example

An organisation has following total costs at different activity levels.

Activity level (units)	4,000	6,000	8,000
Total cost ($)	105,000	150,000	190,000

There is a 20% step increase in fixed costs for each increase in activity level of 5,000 units.

Find the total cost of 4,500 units.

Solution

Calculate the variable cost per unit using two activity levels for which the fixed costs are the same. For example, both the 6,000 and 8,000 levels are within the 5,000 to 10,000 range:

Variable cost per unit = (190,000 – 150,000) / (8,000 – 6,000) = $20

Total fixed cost above 5,000 units = 190,000 – 8,000 × 20 = $30,000

Total fixed cost below 5,000 units = 30,000 × 100/120 = 25,000

Total cost for 4,500 units = 25,000 + 4,500 × 20 = $115,000

Cost equations

Cost equations can be derived from historic data and then used to estimate future costs.

The total cost $y = a + bx$ where:

a = fixed cost per period
b = variable cost per unit
x = activity level

If fixed cost per period = $3,000 and variable cost per unit = $5

Then total cost per period $y = 3,000 + 5x$

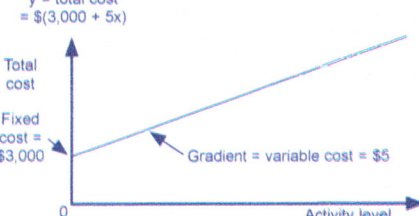

Example

The total cost of a product is given by the equation $y = 4,500 + 3.5x$.

The total fixed cost is $4,500

The variable cost is $3.50

The total cost for 100 units is
$(4,500 + 3.5 \times 100) = 4,850$

Cost codes

A code is a system of symbols designed to be applied to a classified set of items, to give a brief accurate reference, which helps entry to the records, collation and analysis.

Coding systems

There are many ways to cost codes. Here are some of the more popular methods:

- Sequential Code – each code follows a numerical or alphabetical sequence.
- Block Code – often used to categorise sequential codes together.
- Hierarchical Code – each digit in the code represents a classification. As the code progresses from left to right each digit represents a smaller subset.
- Significant digit code – is a code that contains individual digits and letters that are used to represent features of the coded item.

- Faceted Code – is a code that is broken down into a number of facets or fields, each of which signifies a unit of information.

3

Accounting for materials

In this chapter

- Inventory control.
- The costs of having inventory.
- Reorder levels.
- Economic order quantity.
- Economic batch quantity.
- Control procedures.
- Valuing inventory.
- Just in Time.
- The materials inventory account.

You need to understand the physical procedures for managing inventory as well as the method used for recording and accounting for it.

Inventory control

Ordering and purchasing

Documentation

Businesses will have computerised systems that will produce or use the following documents to record transactions and movements of material.

Document	Completed by	Sent to	Information included
Purchase requisitions	Stores department	Purchasing department	Goods required

Manager's authorisation |
| Quotation | Supplier | Purchasing department | Cost of goods ordered |
| Purchase order form | Purchasing department | Supplier

Accounting (copy)

Goods receiving department (copy) | Goods required |
| Delivery note | Supplier | Goods receiving department | Check of goods delivered against order form |
| Invoice | Supplier | Accounting | Details of money due |
| Materials requisitions | Production department | Stores | Authorisation to release goods

Update stores records |
| Materials returns | Production department | Stores | Details of goods returned to stores
Update stores records |

| Goods returned | Stores | Supplier | Details of goods returned to stores. Unwanted or damaged |
| Credit note | Supplier | Accounting | Details of goods returned or fault with invoice |

Computerised inventory control systems

Extranet

- Controlled private network.

- Allows access to partners, vendors and suppliers and authorised customers to access information from an organisation's intranet.

Transaction Processing Systems (TPS)

- Records historic information and represents the simple automation of previously manual systems.

- Captures, processes, stores and outputs the low-level transaction data.

- Records all the daily transactions of the organisation and summarises them so they can be reported on a routine basis.

Management information systems (MIS)

- Converts internal and external data into useful information that is then communicated to managers at all levels and across all functions to enable them to make timely and effective decisions for planning and controlling activities.

- Will collate information from individual transactions recorded in the accounting system to allow middle managers to control the business.

- Customer purchases are summarised into reports to identify the products and customers providing the most revenue.

You need to understand the costs associated with holding inventory and be able to calculate economic order quantities with and without discounts. The formulae will be given but make sure that you know how to use them.

The costs of having inventory

Holding costs – costs associated with holding inventory.

Holding costs	
Fixed holding costs	**Variable holding costs**
Cost of storage space	Interest on capital tied up in inventory
Cost of insurance	

Ordering costs – costs associated with placing orders.

- Administrative costs.

- Delivery costs.

- Order costs vary with number of orders placed.

Main objective of inventory control is to minimise total of holding, ordering and stock-out costs.

Total annual cost of inventory = Purchase cost × Annual demand + Cost of placing an order × number of orders + holding cost per unit of inventory × average inventory

$$TAC = PD + (Co × D/Q) + (Ch × Q/2)$$

Reorder levels

Definition

Reorder level is the predetermined level of inventory at which order is placed.

To avoid the risk of stock-outs when demand during lead time to delivery is constant:

Reorder level = usage × lead time

When lead time and demand in lead time is not constant:

Reorder level = maximum usage × maximum lead time

Maximum inventory level = reorder level + reorder quantity – (minimum usage × minimum lead time)

Minimum inventory level (**buffer or safety stock**) = reorder level – (average usage × average lead time)

Average inventory = (reorder quantity / 2) + minimum inventory

Economic order quantity

The economic order quantity minimises the total of ordering and holding costs.

Economic order quantity = $Q = \sqrt{\dfrac{2C_O D}{C_H}}$

Where:

D = demand per annum

C_O = cost of placing one order

C_H = cost of holding one unit per year

Annual ordering costs = $C_O \times D/Q$

Annual holding cost = $C_H \times Q/2$
(because it is assumed that average stock is half the order quantity)

Example

Annual demand = 125,000 units

Ordering cost = $10 per order

Holding cost = $0.10 per unit per annum

EOQ = $\sqrt{(2 \times 10 \times 125{,}000/0.10)}$ = 5,000 units

The EOQ with discounts for bulk ordering (bulk discounts)

Calculate the EOQ without discount

If EOQ is smaller than minimum for discount, calculate total annual costs of holding, ordering and purchase costs for EOQ

Calculate total costs for a reorder quantity just large enough to qualify for bulk discount

Compare total costs for both order quantities and select minimum cost alternative

Economic batch quantity

The economic batch quantity considers the number of manufactured items which should be produced in a batch to minimise the total costs.

- Cost of holding inventory.
- Cost of setting up batch ready for production.

$$EBQ = Q = \sqrt{\dfrac{2C_O D}{C_H\left(1 - \dfrac{D}{R}\right)}}$$

Where:

D = demand per annum

C_O = cost of setting up batch

C_H = cost of holding one unit per year

R = annual replenishment (annual production) rate

Annual setup costs = $C_O \times D/Q$

Annual holding cost = $C_H \times Q/2(1 - D/R)$

Control procedures

Perpetual inventory	Recording, as they occur, receipts, issues and the resulting balances of individual items of inventory in either quantity or quantity and value.
Periodic stocktaking	Checking balance of every item of inventory on the same date, usually at the end of an accounting period.
Continuous stocktaking	Counting and valuing selected items of inventory on a rotating basis. Specialist teams count and check certain inventory items on each day.
Slow-moving inventory	Those inventory items which take a long time to be used up.
Obsolete inventory	Those items of inventory which have become out of date and are no longer required.
Stores ledger card	Card used to update inventory records showing receipts, issues and orders.

Other control procedures include:

- use of standard costs
- separation of ordering and purchasing
- checking all goods received
- delivery signatures
- physical security procedures.

Valuing inventory

FIFO (first in, first out)

Assumes that issues will be made from the oldest inventory available, leaving the latest purchases in inventory.

LIFO (last in, first out)

Assumes that issues will be made from the newest inventory available, leaving the earliest purchases in inventory.

Weighted average cost (AVCO)

Weighted average cost = Total cost of items in inventory/Number of items in inventory. Takes account of the relative quantities purchased at different prices in the cost per unit.

Just in Time

- Goods and services should be produced only when they are needed.

- Aims to have zero inventories of raw materials, work in progress or finished goods.

JIT production is driven by demand for finished products whereby each component on a production line is produced only when needed for the next stage.

JIT purchasing is where material purchases are contracted so that the receipt and usage of material coincide.

To be able to operate a JIT system there are a number of requirements:

- High quality – materials and the production system must be reliable.

- Speed – the production system must be fast to enable customer orders to be met when placed.

- Flexibility – the production system must be able to respond immediately to customer orders and be flexible to order size.

The materials inventory account

Materials inventory account	
Debit entries – increase in inventory	**Credit entries – decrease in inventory**
Opening inventory (opening balance)	Work-in-progress (direct materials used)
Payables (materials purchased on credit)	Materials returned to suppliers
	Production overheads (indirect materials used)
Materials returned to stores	Statement of profit or loss (material write-offs)
	Closing inventory (closing balance)

Item	Debit entry	Credit entry
Materials purchased on credit	Materials inventory account	Payables
Materials returned to stores	Materials inventory account	Work-in-progress account
Direct materials used in production	Work-in-progress account	Materials inventory account
Materials returned to suppliers	Payables	Materials inventory account
Indirect materials used	Production overheads	Materials inventory account
Materials written-off	Statement of profit or loss	Materials inventory account

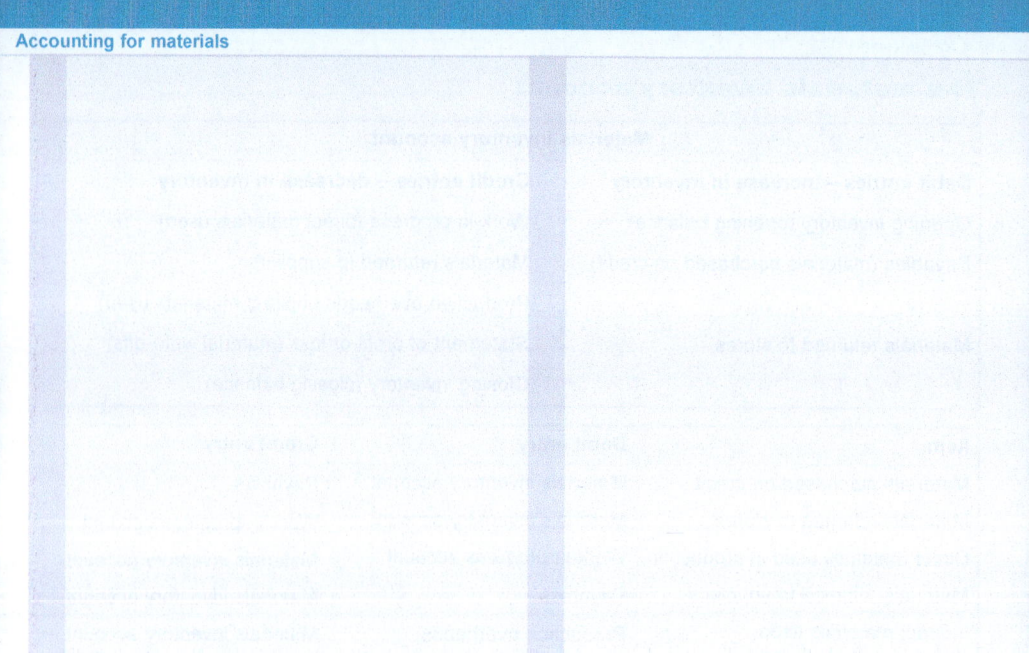

4

Accounting for labour

In this chapter

- Remuneration methods.
- Direct and indirect labour costs.
- Accounting for labour costs.
- Labour ratios.

There are two key areas when considering labour costs:

- determining the wages bill to be paid

- splitting the labour cost between its direct and indirect elements.

Specific details of remuneration schemes will be given in the question. Read it carefully and do exactly what it says.

Remuneration methods

The specific details of schemes will be given in the question. Read it carefully.

Time based schemes

Total wages = (hours worked × basic rate of pay per hour) + (overtime hours worked × overtime premium per hour).

Time based schemes:

- can result in higher quality as workers are happy to spend longer on units to get them right

- some workers may take longer just to get paid more. There is no incentive to improve productivity.

Piecework schemes

Total wages = number of units completed × agreed rate per unit.

Piecework schemes:

- may involve a guaranteed minimum wage

- may use higher rate per unit once productivity target is achieved

- may result in higher productivity at the expense of quality.

Other schemes

Many involve flat salary plus bonus.

Bonus schemes

- Can be aimed at individuals and/ or groups.

- Use many different systems.

Direct and indirect labour costs

Type of worker	Direct labour cost	Indirect labour cost
Workers directly involved in making products	Basic pay Overtime premium on specific job at customer's request	General overtime premium Bonus payments Idle time Sick pay Time spent on indirect jobs
Indirect workers • Maintenance staff • Supervisors • Canteen staff		All costs

Accounting for labour costs

Labour account	
Debit entry	**Credit entries**
Bank – labour costs incurred	Work-in-progress – direct labour costs
	Production overheads – indirect labour costs

Example

A company operates a premium bonus scheme for its employees of 50% of the time saved compared with the standard time allowance for a job, at the normal hourly rate. The data relating to Job 999 completed by an employee is as follows:

Allowed time for Job 999 12 hours

Time taken to complete Job 999 10 hours

Normal hourly rate of pay $15

What is the total pay of the employee for the 10 hours spent on Job 999?

Solution

Time saved = 12 – 10 = 2 hours

Bonus paid = $0.50 × 2 hours × $15 = $15

Basic pay for time worked=10 hours × $15 =$150

Total pay −$165

Labour ratios

Labour turnover is a measure of the proportion of people leaving compared to those employed.

Labour turnover for a given period =

$$\frac{\text{Number of leavers who require replacement}}{\text{Average number of employees}} \times 100\%$$

Labour efficiency ratio measures performance by comparing actual time taken to do the job with the expected time.

Labour efficiency ratio =

$$\frac{\text{Standard hours worked to produce actual output}}{\text{Actual hours worked to produce actual output}} \times 100\%$$

Definition

Labour capacity ratio compares numbers of hours spent actively working with total hours available.

Labour capacity ratio =

$$\frac{\text{Actual hours worked to produce actual output}}{\text{Total budgeted hours}} \times 100\%$$

Definition

Labour production volume ratio compares numbers of hours expected to be worked to produce actual output with total hours available for work.

Labour production volume ratio =

$$\frac{\text{Standard hours to produce actual output}}{\text{Total budgeted hours}} \times 100\%$$

Definition

Standard hour = A standard hour can be used to state the number of production units which should be achieved within a period of one hour.

Example

Actual output in period	250 units
Actual hours worked	420 hours
Standard time allowed per unit	90 minutes
Budgeted hours	450 hours

Solution

Standard hours to make actual output
= 250 units × 90/60 = 375 hours

Labour efficiency ratio = 375/420 × 100
= 89%

Labour capacity ratio = 420/450 × 100 = 93%

Labour production volume ratio = 375/450 × 100 = 83%

5

Accounting for overheads

In this chapter

- Overheads and absorption costing.
- Cost allocation and apportionment.
- Reapportionment.
- Absorption.
- Under- and over-absorption.
- Accounting for production overheads.

If a question asks you to calculate the total cost of a product, deal with the direct costs and then the overheads.

When a question asks about overheads, check how much of the following diagram needs to be worked through.

You may also need to understand how to choose a suitable base for apportionment.

Step 1:
Overheads allocated or apportioned to cost centres using suitable bases

Budgeted production overheads

Cost centres A   B   C   D

Production departments

Service departments

Step 2:
Service centre costs reapportioned to production centres

Step 3:
Overheads absorbed into units of production

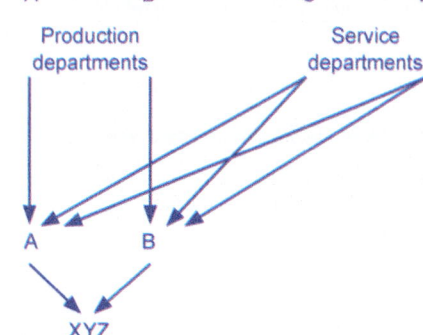

A   B

Units of production   XYZ

Overheads and absorption costing

Definition

Overheads are indirect costs which cannot be identified to a particular cost unit or cost centre.

- Overheads may be fixed or variable.

Definition

Absorption costing is the process by which production overheads are recovered by absorbing them into a product by a three stage process:

- allocation and apportionment of overheads

- reapportionment of service cost centre overheads

- absorption of overheads.

Cost allocation and apportionment

Definition

Allocation is the charging of overheads directly to specific departments where they can be identified directly with a cost centre or cost unit.

Definition

Apportionment is the sharing of overheads which relate to more than one department between those departments on a fair basis.

- The apportionment should be in proportion to the benefit received.

Reapportionment

Service department costs need to be reapportioned to the production departments.

- This should be done using a suitable basis linked to usage of the service.

- Step down apportionment is used when one service department works or provides a service for other service departments as well as the production departments. The service department that provides services for more departments is reapportioned first.

- The main complication here is having multiple service departments with reciprocal usage. The easiest way to deal with this is to repeatedly reapportion overheads out of service departments until the figures are no longer material.

Example of reciprocal apportionment

The total overheads allocated and apportioned to the production and service departments of LS Ltd are as follows.

Assembly = $17,350

Finishing = $23,970

Maintenance = $18,600

Canteen = $6,600

A suitable basis for sharing out the maintenance costs is the time spent servicing equipment. The amount of time spent by the maintenance department servicing equipment in the other three departments has been analysed as follows.

Assembly	50%
Finishing	40%
Canteen	10%

The Canteen department's overheads are to be reapportioned on the basis of the number of employees in the other three departments.

	Assembly	Finishing	Maintenance	Canteen
Number of employees	18	30	12	2

Solution

	Assembly $	Finishing $	Maintenance $	Canteen $	Total $
Total from above	17,350	23,970	18,600	6,600	66,520
Reapportion canteen	1,980	3,300	1,320	(6,600)	–
Reapportion maintenance	9,960	7,968	(19,920)	1,992	–
Reapportion canteen	598	996	398	(1,992)	–
Reapportion maintenance	199	159	(398)	40	–
Reapportion canteen	12	20	8	(40)	–
Reapportion maintenance	4	3	(8)	1	–
Reapportion canteen	0	1	–	(1)	–
Total	30,103	36,417	0	0	66,520

Absorption

Definition

Absorption is the process whereby costs within cost centres are charged to a cost unit.

Different bases can be used:

- labour or machine hours (the most common approach)
- percentage of direct labour cost
- percentage of material cost
- percentage of prime cost
- cost per unit (gives a blanket overhead cost per unit for all products).

Overhead absorption rate = OAR = budgeted overheads / budgeted level of activity.

Under and over-absorption

If overheads are absorbed throughout a period using the predetermined overhead absorption rate, at the end of the period there may be a difference between the overheads absorbed and the actual overhead incurred.

Using direct labour hours:

Overhead absorbed = actual direct labour hours × OAR	X
Actual overhead incurred	X
Difference = overhead under- or over-absorbed	?

There are two main reasons for this difference:

- actual overheads different from budget
- actual activity level different from budget.

If overheads have been under-absorbed, then they have not all been accounted for and an additional debit is needed in the statement of profit or loss to account for the difference.

If overheads have been over-absorbed, then too high a value of overheads has been accounted for and an additional credit is needed in the statement of profit or loss to cancel out that effect.

Exam focus

Sometimes you may be given information relating to the actual **under-absorption** or **over-absorption** in a period and be expected to calculate the budgeted overheads or the actual number of hours worked. As long as you remember the basic formula involved in calculating under- or over-absorption, you shouldn't have any problems.

Accounting for production overheads

Production Overheads

	£		£
Actual Overhead cost (1)		Absorbed overheads (2)	
Over-absorbed (3)		Under-absorbed (4)	

(1) The **actual cost** of all the indirect costs is recorded as a **debit** in the production overheads account. The credit is either in the bank or payables account. The actual cost will be made up of all the indirect production costs – material, labour and expenses.

(2) The overheads that are **absorbed into production** (WIP) are recorded as a **credit** in the production overheads account. This is calculated as the **budgeted OAR × actual activity.**

(3) When the account is balanced at the end of the period and the **balancing amount** is required to make the **debit** side of the account match the credit side we have an **over-absorption** of overheads.

(4) When the account is balanced at the end of the period and the **balancing amount** is required to make the **credit** side of the account match the debit side we have an **under-absorption** of overheads.

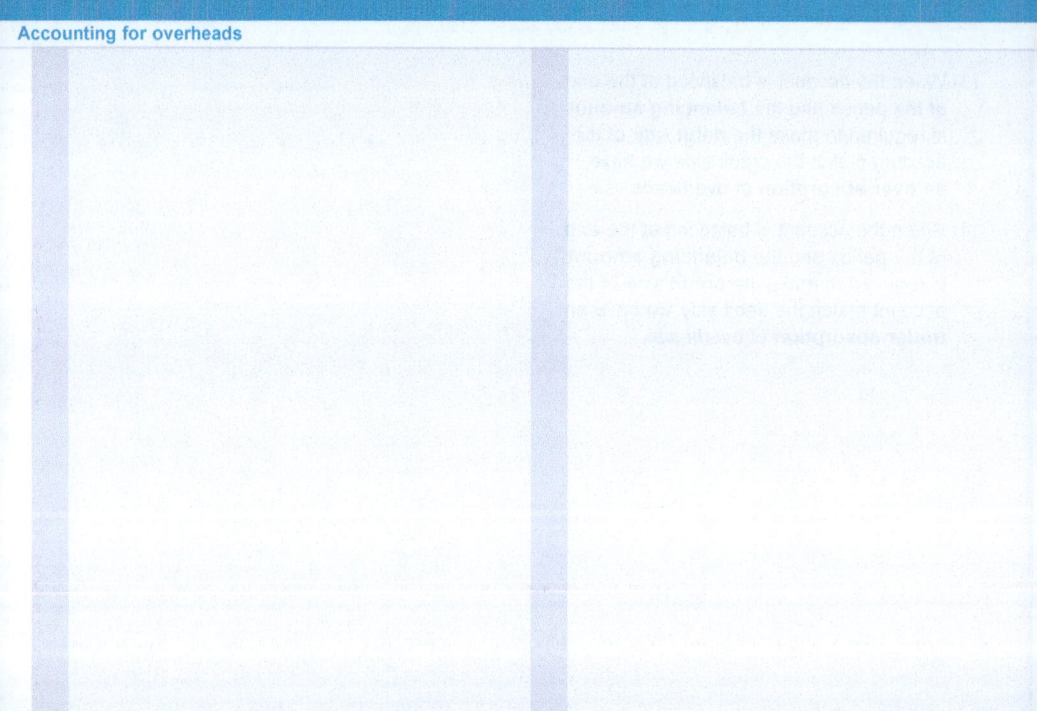

chapter

Absorption and marginal costing

In this chapter

- The concept of contribution.
- Absorption and marginal costing.
- Arguments for the different approaches.

The concept of contribution is very important as this is at the heart of marginal costing and the decision-making process. You also need to be able to reconcile the different profit figures using marginal and absorption costing.

The concept of contribution

Definition

The marginal cost of a unit of product is the total of the variable costs of the product.

- It is the additional cost of producing an extra unit of the product.

Definition

Contribution = sales price – variable cost
Profit = contribution – fixed cost

Contribution per unit of product:

- gives an idea of how much money there is available to contribute towards paying for the overheads of the organisation

- is usually assumed to be constant at varying levels of output and sales.

Absorption and marginal costing

	Absorption costing	**Marginal costing**
Valuing units	Units are valued at total production cost	Units are valued at marginal (variable production) cost
Valuing inventory	Opening and closing inventory are valued at total production cost	Opening and closing inventory are valued at marginal cost
Treatment of fixed production overheads	Carried forward from one period to another as part of the closing (opening) inventory valuation. They only hit the profit figure when units are sold	Fixed costs are charged in full against profit in the period in which they are incurred
Adjusting for under- or over-absorption	An adjustment for under- or over-absorption of overheads is made in the statement of profit or loss	No adjustment for under- or over-absorption of overheads needed

	Absorption costing	Marginal costing
Impact of increase in inventory level	Gives higher profit	Gives lower profit
Impact of decrease in inventory level	Gives lower profit	Gives higher profit
Inventory level constant	Same profit with both systems	

Note: the difference in profit is due solely to the different opening and closing inventory values, which is due to the treatment of fixed production overheads. It has nothing to do with under- or over-absorption of overheads.

Reconciliation statement

Absorption costing profit	X
Change in inventory × FOAR	+/-X
Marginal costing profit	X

Marginal costing profit statement

Sales revenue = units sold × price	X
Less cost of sales = units sold × marginal cost of a unit	(X)
Less variable non-production costs actually incurred	(X)
Contribution	XX
Less fixed production costs actually incurred	(X)
Less fixed non-production costs actually incurred	(X)
Net profit/(loss)	XX

Absorption costing profit statement

Sales revenue = units sold × price	X
Less cost of sales = units sold × full production cost of a unit	(X)
Over/ (under) absorption	X
Gross profit	XX
Less variable non-production costs actually incurred	(X)
Less fixed non-production costs actually incurred	(X)
Net profit/(loss)	XX

Arguments for the different approaches

Advantages of marginal costing	Advantages of absorption costing
• Contribution per unit is constant unlike profit per unit which varies with changes in sales volumes.	• Absorption costing includes an element of fixed overheads in inventory values (in accordance with accounting standards).
• There is no under or over absorption of overheads (and hence no adjustment is required in the statement of profit or loss).	• Analysing under/over absorption of overheads is a useful exercise in controlling costs of an organisation.
• Fixed costs are a period cost and are charged in full to the period under consideration.	• In small organisations, absorbing overheads into the costs of products is the best way of estimating job costs and profits on jobs.
• Marginal costing is useful in the decision making process.	
• It is simple to operate.	

7

Job, batch and process costing

In this chapter

- Job costing.
- Batch costing.
- Process costing.
- Joint and by-products.

The key to service, job and batch costing is to treat them like any other normal costing exercise – deal with direct costs first and then look at how to apportion/absorb overheads.

Job costing

The key feature of job costing is that each job is unique.

- Produce a cost card for each individual job to find out the costs that will be incurred.

- All the same principles of costing should be used.

The total cost of the job is made up as:

	$
Direct materials	X
Direct labour	X
Direct expenses	X
Overheads absorbed	X
TOTAL COST	XX

Profit may be a mark-up on cost or a margin (percentage of price).

- Check carefully to make sure you are using the correct formula.

Batch costing

The key feature of batch costing is that each batch is different, but within each batch all items are identical.

The costing process has two steps.

1 Determine the total cost of the batch, effectively treating each batch as a job in its own right.

2 Cost per unit = total batch costs / number of units in the batch.

Some costs, such as design or set-up costs, may be fixed regardless of the size of the batch; others will vary with the number of units in the batch.

Process costing

Process costing is used where production is continuous, making it difficult to identify conventional, separate units of production.

A series of separate processes is required to manufacture the finished product. The output of one process becomes the input of the next process.

There are often losses in the process, so output from a process does not equal input.

There may be by-products and joint products.

Normal losses

A **normal loss** is one that is expected to occur.

Example

Input 1,000 units.

Normal loss equal to 5% of input, giving a normal loss of 50 units.

Input 1,000 units = Output 950 units + Normal loss 50 units

Abnormal loss

An **abnormal loss** occurs when actual losses are greater than expected losses.

Example

Input 1,000 units

Normal loss is 5% of input

Output is 940 units

There would therefore be 10 units of abnormal loss.

Input 1,000 units = Output 940 units + Normal loss 50 units + Abnormal loss 10 units

Abnormal gain

An abnormal gain occurs when the actual loss in period is less than expected.

Example

Input 1,000 units

Normal loss is 5% of input

Output is 960 unit

There would therefore be 10 units of abnormal gain.

Input 1,000 units + Abnormal gain 10 units = Output 960 units + Normal loss 50 units

Joint and by-products

Definition

Joint products are:

- two or more products, indistinguishable until the split-off point, each having a sufficiently high saleable value to be recognised as a main product

- costs before the split-off point are common to all products and are called **joint costs** or **common costs**.

Definition

By-products are:

- output of insignificant value produced with joint products.

Accounting treatment

Joint products	By-products

• Joint costs apportioned between the joint products at split-off point to obtain the cost of each product to value inventory and cost of sales
 	
• Basis of apportionment usually one of:
  – sales value of production
  – production units
  – net realisable value
	Non-cost methods
	• Other income – The net sales of by-products for the current period is recognised as Other Income.
	• By-product revenue deducted from the main product(s) cost – The net sales of value of the by-products will be treated as a deduction from the cost of the main product.
	
	Cost Methods of Accounting for By-Products
	• Replacement Cost Method values the by-product inventory at its opportunity cost of purchasing or replacing the by-products.
	• Total Costs Less By-Products Valued at Standard Price Method – By-products are valued at a standard price to avoid fluctuations in by-product value.
	• Joint Cost Pro-rata Method allocates some of the joint cost to the by-product using any one of the joint cost allocation methods. This method is rarely used in practice.

Example

A company produces two joint products, A and B, and one by-product C. There are no costs specifically identifiable to product B:

	$	$	$
	A	**B**	**Total**
Revenue	X	X	X
Costs identifiable to individual products	(X)	–	(X)
Net realisable value	XX	XX	XX
Common costs less profit from the by-product	(X)	(X)	(X)
Profit	XX	XX	XX

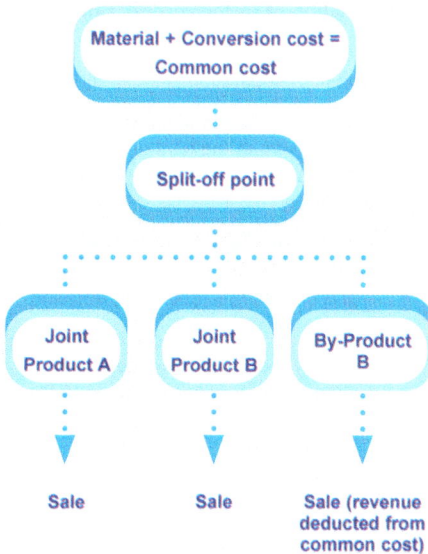

Material + Conversion cost = Common cost

Split-off point

Joint Product A

Joint Product B

By-Product B

Sale

Sale

Sale (revenue deducted from common cost)

Evaluation of further processing

- further processing of products after the point of separation is independent

- pre-split off costs of the common processing of the joint products are irrelevant to the further processing decision

- joint costs are not affected by whether individual products are further processed, and are not relevant to the decision under consideration

- identify the incremental costs and incremental revenues relating to that further processing.

Service and operation costing

In this chapter

- The nature of service and operation costing.
- Suitable cost units.
- Service cost analysis.

Determining costs for services is just like any other costing exercise but with the added complication of the selection of a suitable cost unit.

The nature of service and operation costing

Four main differences between the output of **service industries** and products of manufacturing industries:

- intangibility – output cannot be touched or examined

- heterogeneity – nature of output is variable due to high human input and the nature of many services

- simultaneous production and consumption – service cannot be inspected before receiving it

- perishability – services cannot be stored.

Suitable cost units

There are no set rules for selecting service cost units.

- cost units should be based on their relevance to the service provided

- may be necessary to use composite cost units

- it is often useful in service organisations to calculate more than one different type of cost unit to enable cost control.

Example

Service	Possible cost unit
Hotel	Cost per guest per night
Transport	Cost per passenger mile
College	Cost per student
Hospital	Cost per patient day
	Cost per procedure

Service cost analysis

All the same principles of costing should be used. This means that the total cost per unit (whatever the unit happens to be) is still made up as:

	$
Direct materials	X
Direct labour	X
Direct expenses	X
Overheads absorbed	X
TOTAL COST	XX

$$\text{Cost per service unit} = \frac{\text{Total costs for providing service}}{\text{Number of service units used to provide the service}}$$

The key characteristics of service product costs are:

- labour may be the only direct cost

- overheads usually make up the bulk of the cost and are likely to be absorbed using direct labour hours.

9

Alternative costing principles

In this chapter

- Activity based costing.
- Target costing.
- Life cycle costing.
- Product life cycle.

This chapter covers some alternative forms of costing. It is important to understand the concepts for each of these.

Activity based costing

ABC is a form of absorption costing but rather than absorbing overheads on a production volume basis (such as hours worked) it allocates costs into cost pools and then absorbs them using cost drivers.

Cost pool – an activity that consumes resources and for which overhead costs are identified and allocated.

Cost driver – a unit of activity that consumes resources or the factor that influences the level of cost.

Advantages	Disadvantages
• More accurate cost per unit	• Only of benefit is overheads are significant
• Better pricing strategy	• Some arbitrary allocation will still have to made
• More information on what causes a cost	• Complex procedure therefore time consuming and costly
• Can be applied to all overheads not just production overheads	

Target costing

Is a cost estimate derived by subtracting a desired profit from a competitive market price. Often cost will need to be reduced to be able to achieve the target.

Value analysis is a systematic examination of factors affecting the cost of a product or service, in order to devise means of achieving the specified purpose most economically.

Value engineering attempts to design the best possible value at the lowest possible cost into a new product.

Life cycle costing

This technique compares the revenues from a product with all the costs incurred over the entire product life cycle. This enables:

- Profitability to be forecast for a product over its entire life.
- Costs to be compared at any stage of the products life cycle.

Product life cycle
Sales/profit

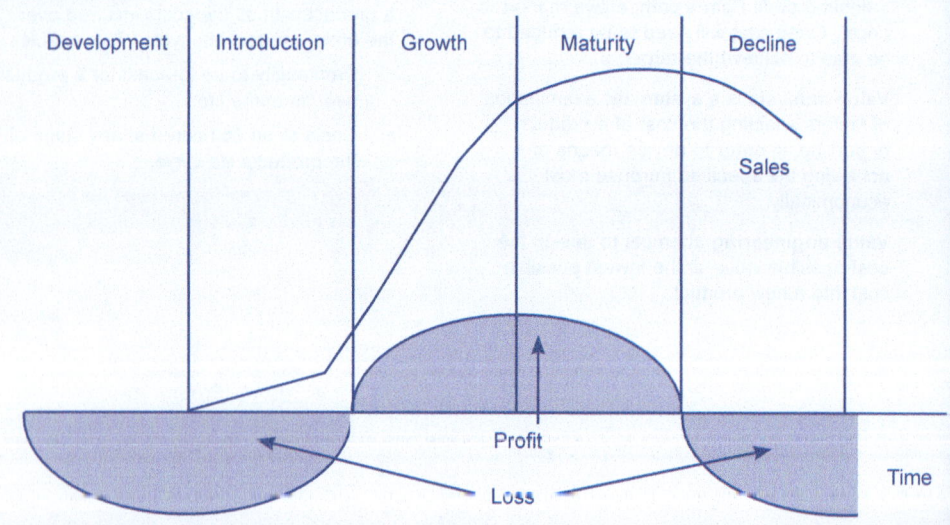

10

Sources of data

In this chapter

- Types of data.
- Sources of data.
- Sampling techniques.
- Big data.

It is important that you understand where information can be sourced from. It is also important to be able to identify which sampling technique would be most appropriate when.

Types of data

Primary data is data that is obtained directly from first-hand sources by means of surveys, observation or experimentation. It is data that has not been previously published. Primary data is any data which is used solely for the purpose for which it was originally collected.

Secondary data is any information that has been collected or researched recently. Sources of secondary data include the internet, libraries, company reports, newspaper, governments and banks. The data collected is useful as it allows the researcher to see the other opinions on their area of study but care must be taken that the data is reliable and accurate. Secondary data is data that has already been collected for some other purpose but can also be used for the purpose in hand.

- Numerical data – discrete and continuous data
- Categorical data – nominal and ordinal data
- Data analysis – descriptive and inferential analysis

Sources of data

- Machine/sensor – robots on a production line, location data from a mobile phone
- Transactional – product IDs, payment information, bank data
- Human/social – social media

Internal sources

- Accounting system
- Payroll system
- Planning system

Benefits

- Readily available
- Easy to sort and analyse
- Relates to the organisation concerned

Limitations

- May need further processing to be of use

External sources

- Government
- Other businesses
- Trade associations
- Financial and business press
- Internet

Benefits

- Wide expanse
- Easily accessible
- General and specific information available

Limitations

- Accuracy
- Time consuming searches

Data capture costs

The costs of information can be classified as follows:

Costs of internal information

- Direct data capture costs, e.g. the cost of barcode scanners in a supermarket.
- Processing costs, e.g. salaries paid to payroll processing staff.
- Indirect costs, e.g. information collected which is not needed or is duplicated.

Costs of external information

- Direct costs, e.g. newspaper subscriptions.
- Indirect costs e.g. wasted time finding useful information.
- Management costs, e.g. the cost of processing information.
- Infrastructure costs, e.g. of systems enabling internet searches.

Indirect costs of producing information

The cost of labour – collecting data, inputting data into the system, processing the data and outputting the resulting information. The company needs to pay wages so labour becomes part of the cost of producing information.

Training is expensive in terms of the trainer/ venue, paying wages for people being trained, paying the wages for someone to do the normal work for the person being trained.

Examples of other indirect costs include:

- Loss of staff morale.
- Delays caused in other projects of the business.
- Upsetting customers from system change.
- Incompatibility with other systems.
- Reduced quality of information, due to information overload.
- Poor decision making, due to information overload.
- Too many areas to focus on – so issues are not followed up.

Sampling techniques

Random sampling

A sample is taken in such a way that every member of the population has an equal chance of being selected.

Systematic sampling

The sample is taken by choosing a random initial number and then picking the nth item after that i.e. the first item is chosen as number 12, the next will be 112, then 212, then 312. The frequency of the nth item will depend on how big the sample population is and how many pieces of information are required.

Stratified sampling

The population is split into well defined groups (men and women, age groups etc) then a random sample is taken from each group.

Multi-stage sampling

Used if a population is very large – for example if a sample was required from a whole country (i.e. during a government election) the process would be:

1   The country is divided into areas and random sample is taken.

2   Each sampled area (from 1) is divided into towns/cities and a random sample is taken.

3   Each town/city (from 2) is divided into roads and a random sample is taken.

4   From each road (from 3) random houses are sampled and the occupants questioned.

Cluster sampling

Similar to multi-stage sampling but once the desired number of areas are chosen every occupant in that area would be part of the sample.

Quota sampling

The interviewer knows how many 'types' need to be interviewed i.e. 20 males between 20 and 29 years old. The interviewer will use any method to reach the sample size.

Big data

Definition

Extremely large collections of data that may be analysed to reveal patterns, trends and associations.

The processing of Big Data is known as Big Data analytics, for example using Hadoop software.

Characterised by the 5Vs

Volume	Organisations now hold huge volumes of data, for example on customer purchases.
Variety	Data can be financial or non-financial, internal or external, structured, unstructured, semi-structured.
Velocity	The data needs to be turned into useful information quickly.
Veracity	Is the data accurate enough?
Value	Does the data add value?

Analysing data

In this chapter

- Averaging data and measures of spread.
- Averaging data example.
- Measures of spread example.
- Risk and uncertainty.
- Expected values and probability.
- Normal distribution.

Averaging data and measures of spread

Averaging measures

Spread measures

> **Mean**
> This is the average found by dividing the sum of values by the number of values.

> **Standard deviation and variance**
> These are measures of how far the data points are from the mean.
> variance = standard deviation^2

> **Median**
> This is the middle value of a set of values.

> **Coefficient of variation**
> This means a measure of the dispersion of the data points around the mean.
> Calculated as:
>
> $$\frac{\text{standard deviation}}{\text{mean}}$$

> **Mode**
> This is the value which occurs most often.

Averaging data example

Sample data: 1,120, 990, 1,040, 1,030, 1,105, 1,015

Mean = $\dfrac{\Sigma x}{n}$ = $\dfrac{6,300}{6}$ = $\underline{1,050}$

Median = middle observation

990, 1,015, 1,030, 1,040, 1,105, 1,120

median = $\dfrac{1,030 + 1,040}{2}$ = 1,035

Frequency distribution

Output	f	x	fx
350-360	4	355	1,420
360-370	6	365	2,190
370-380	5	375	1,875
380-390	4	385	1,540
390-400	3	395	1,185
	22		8,210

x = midpoint of class

Mean = $\dfrac{\Sigma fx}{\Sigma f}$ = $\dfrac{8,210}{22}$ = $\underline{373}$

Measures of spread example

Standard deviation

Σ	f	fx	fx^2
2	2	4	8
3	4	12	36
4	3	12	48
5	4	20	100
6	3	18	108
7	3	21	147
8	3	24	192
	22	111	639

$$sd = \sqrt{\frac{\Sigma fx^2}{\Sigma f} - \left(\frac{\Sigma fx}{\Sigma f}\right)^2}$$

$$= \sqrt{\frac{639}{22} - 5,045^2} = 1.9$$

Variance = standard deviation^2

$$= 1.9^2 = 3.61$$

Coefficient of variation

Coefficient of variation = $\dfrac{\text{standard deviation}}{\text{mean}}$

$$= \frac{1.9}{5.045} = 38\%$$

mean $= \dfrac{\Sigma fx}{\Sigma f} = \dfrac{111}{22} = 5.045$

Risk and uncertainty

RISK describes a situation where we know the different possible outcomes and can estimate their associated probabilities.

UNCERTAINTY is used when we do not know the possible outcomes and/or their associated probabilities. Uncertainty is essentially a matter of ignorance.

Expected values and probability

Probability is the likelihood of a given event occurring

If we can compile a complete list of all the equally likely outcomes, we can define the probability of an event, denoted P (event), as

$$P \text{ (event)} = \frac{\text{total number of outcomes which constitute the event}}{\text{total number of possible outcomes}}$$

Features of probability
• all lie between 0 (impossible) and 1 (certain)
• P (not A) = 1 − P (A)

Expected value is a long – run average

If an action has outcomes (x) with associated probabilities (p)

Expected value (EV) = Σpx

Example – daily sales figures

Sales (X)	probability	px
0	0.1	0
1	0.4	0.4
2	0.5	1.0
	1.0	1.4

The expected value is 1.4 sales

Normal distribution

If we know the mean and the standard deviation, we can use the normal distribution to work out the percentage chance of a value occurring.

Convert your variable to a **standard normal variable**

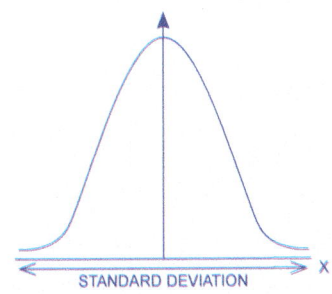

This has:
  Mean (μ) = 0
  Standard deviation (σ) = 1

STANDARD DEVIATION

$$Z = \frac{x - \mu}{\sigma}$$

Where:
  Z = Z score
  X = Value being considered

Features:
  • Bell shaped
  • Symmetrical
  • Mean in the centre
  • Total area under curve = 1

Standard normal curve

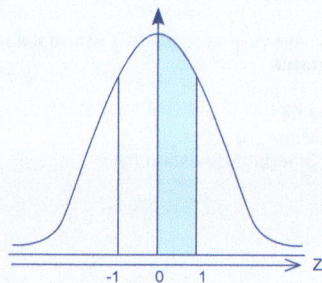

If Z score = 1
From the normal distribution
table = 0.3413 or 34.13%

So, 34.13% is the area from 0 to 1

It is also the area from −1 to 0

Example:

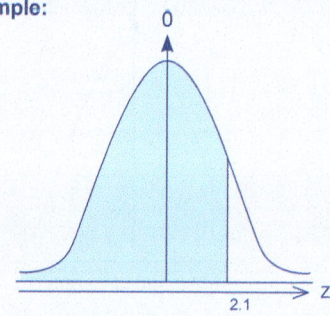

Find the probability that Z score is negative or less than 2.1

$$P(Z < 2.1) = 0.5 + TE\ (2.1)$$
$$= 0.5 + 0.4821$$
$$= 0.9821 = 98.21\%$$

(TE – table entry)

Analytic techniques in budgeting and forecasting

In this chapter

- Regression analysis.
- Time series analysis.
- Index numbers.

You will be given the formulae for regression analysis however it is important that you also understand the significance of each of the variables used and the meaning of r and r^2. You will need to know how to smooth out actual data to give a trend line using time series analysis (moving averages) and also how to adjust data using index numbers.

Regression analysis

Regression

Definition

Given 2 variables, x (independent variable), and y (dependent variable), least squares regression is a way of finding the line of best fit through the scatter diagram.

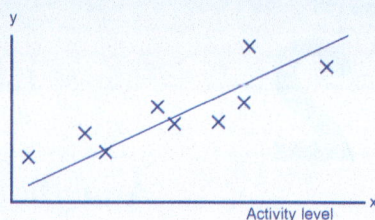

The equation of the line of best fit is:

$y = a + bx$

where a is the y value when x is 0, and b is the change in y when x increases by one unit.

In the context of cost estimation:

y represents the total cost

x represents the production volume in units

a represents the total fixed cost

b represents the variable cost per unit.

To find a and b, use the following formulae (both given):

$$b = \frac{n\sum xy - \sum x \sum y}{n\sum x^2 - (\sum x)^2} \text{ and } a = \frac{\sum y}{n} - b\frac{\sum x}{n}$$

Correlation coefficient (r)

Definition

r measures the strength of a linear relationship between 2 variables.

- The **correlation coefficient** can only take values between -1 and +1
- A value of +1 indicates perfect positive correlation
- A value of 0 indicates no correlation
- A value of -1 indicates perfect negative correlation
- A high correlation coefficient does not prove a causal relationship.

To find r (formula given)

$$r = \frac{n\sum xy - \sum x \sum y}{\sqrt{[n\sum x^2 - (\sum x)^2][n\sum y^2 - (\sum y)^2]}}$$

Coefficient of determination (r^2)

Definition

r^2 is the square of the correlation coefficient. It shows how much of the variation in the dependent variable is explained by the variation in the independent variable.

The rest of the variation is due to:

- random fluctutations, or
- other specific factors not identified.

Note: 'spurious correlation' can occur when there appears to be correlation but the changes in both sets of figures are due to a third factor.

Example

If r = 0.95, r^2 = 0.90 or 90%

This means that 90% of the variation in the dependent variable is explained by the variation in the independent variable.

Time series analysis

Time series analysis is a term used to describe techniques for analysing a time series, in order to:

- identify whether there is any underlying historical trend and if there is, measure it

- use this analysis of the historical trend to forecast the trend into the future

- identify whether there are any seasonal variations around the trend, and if there is measure them

- apply estimated seasonal variations to a trend line forecast in order to prepare a forecast season by season.

A time series has 4 components:

- **Trend** – upwards, downwards or sideways.

- **Seasonal variations** – short term fluctuations in value due to different circumstances which occur at different times of the year, on different days of the week, different times of day.

- **Cyclical variations** – medium term to long term influences usually associated with the economy. These cycles are rarely of consistent length. Cyclical variations are often associated with the economy.

- **Residual or random variations** – is a difference caused by irregular items, which could not be predicted.

Moving averages

A moving average is a series of averages calculated from time series data. It is a technique used to smooth out the peaks and troughs in the data.

Index numbers

An index number is a technique for comparing, over time, changes in some feature of a group of items (e.g. price, quantity consumed, etc) by expressing the property each year as a percentage of some earlier year. The calculation is:

Current period index/base year index × 100

Types of index numbers

- A **simple** index is one that measures the changes in either price or quantity of a single item.
- A **chain base** index number expresses each year's value as a percentage of the value for the previous year.
- A **weighted** index measures the change in overall price or overall quantity of a number of different items compared to the base year.

- Specific examples of weighted index numbers are Laspeyre (uses the base year quantity or price to weight the index) and Paasche (uses the current year quantity or price to weight the index).

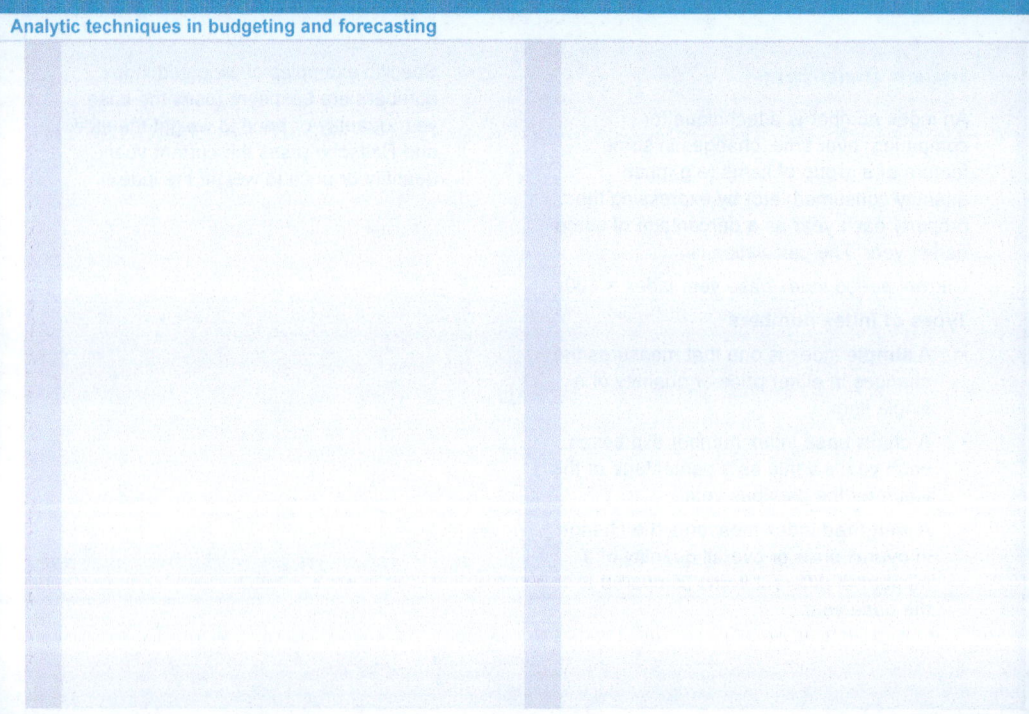

13

Budgeting

In this chapter

- The purpose of budgets.
- Preparing budgets.
- Motivation.
- Incentive schemes.
- Participative budgeting.
- Functional budgets.
- Cash budgets.
- What if analysis.
- Scenario planning.
- Budgetary control cycle.
- Fixed, flexible and flexed budgets.
- Responsibility accounting.
- Controllable and uncontrollable costs.

For the exam you need to understand why budgets are prepared and calculate simple budgets for the various inputs to production. You also need to be able to work with simple flexible and flexed budgets; for this a steady, systematic approach is important.

The purpose of budgets

Definition

A budget is a quantitative expression of a plan of action prepared in advance of the period to which it relates.

- Budgets set out the costs and revenues that are expected to be incurred or earned in future periods.

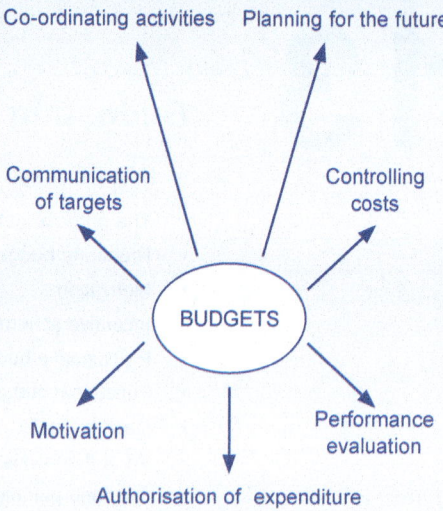

Preparing budgets

Stages in budget preparation

> Define long term objectives of the business

⬇

> Form budget committee to communicate budget policy, set and approve budgets.
>
> Budget committee often includes:
> - Chief executive
> - Budget officer (management accountant)
> - Departmental or functional heads

⬇

> Produce budget manual.
> - Instructions on preparing and using budgets
> - Details of responsibilities – including organisation chart and list of budget holders

⬇

> Identify principal budget factor
> – the limiting factor which limits the activity of the organisation.
> - Usually sales but could be a scarce resource

⬇

> Produce budget for principal budget factor

⬇

> Produce and approve other budgets based on budget for limiting factor

⬇

> Review actual results and compare with budget to calculate variances

Different types of budget

Definition

The master budget includes the budgeted statement of profit or loss, the cash budget and budgeted statement of financial position (balance sheet).

Definition

A continuous budget is a budget which is prepared a year (or budget period) ahead and is updated regularly by adding a further accounting period (month, quarter) when the first accounting period has expired. Continuous budgets are also known as rolling budgets.

Motivation

Motivation is the drive or urge to achieve an end result. An individual is motivated if they are moving forward to achieving goals or objectives.

There is evidence which suggests that management accounting planning and control systems can have a significant effect on manager and employee motivation.

These include:

- the level at which budgets and performance targets are set
- manager and employee reward systems
- the extent to which employees participate in the budget setting process.

Budgets should provide a challenge for employees and managers that is achievable with an appropriate level of effort. The right level of difficulty is that which is acceptable to that individual manager. This level of acceptability will differ from manager to manager, as each individual behaves and reacts in a different way in similar circumstances.

Incentive schemes

Budgets by themselves have a limited motivational effect. It is the reward structure that is linked to achieving the budget requirements, or lack of reward for non-achievement, which provides the real underlying motivational potential of budgets.

Characteristics of a good employee reward system are as follows:

- Fairness
- Motivational
- Understandable
- Consistently applied
- Objective
- Universal

There are three main types of incentive schemes

- Performance related pay (PRP)
- Bonus schemes
- Profit sharing

Participative budgeting

The **top down** approach is where budgets are set by higher levels of management and then communicated to the lower levels of management to whose areas of responsibility they relate. This is also known as an imposed budget.

The **bottom up** approach to budgeting is where lower level managers are involved in setting budget targets. This is known as a participative budget.

Functional budgets

Definition

A functional budget is a budget of income and/or expenditure which applies to a particular function. The main **functional budgets** that you need to be able to prepare are as follows:

- sales budget

- production budget

- raw material usage budget

- raw material purchases budget

- labour budget

- overheads budget.

Sales budget (principal budget factor)		Sales revenue for each product for the period. **Sales budget = expected number of units × planned selling price**
Production budget		Production levels for product to enable budgeted sales volumes. **Budgeted production = forecast sales + closing inventory of finished goods – opening inventory of finished goods**
Material budgets	Usage budget	Material required to produce production levels. Usually expressed as quantity of each material required. **Material usage budget = budgeted production for each product × quantity of material required to produce one unit**
	Purchases budget	Amount of material which needs to be purchased to meet production budget. Usually expressed as quantity and value of material to be purchased. **Material purchases budget = material usage budget + closing inventory – opening inventory**
Labour budget		Cost of labour required to produce budgeted production levels. **Labour budget = number of hours required for the production × labour rate per hour**

Overhead budget		Overhead costs to produce budgeted production levels.
		Budgeted level of activity × standard overhead rate
		Where relevant activity is based on activity over which overheads are apportioned e.g. machine hours to produce budgeted production × production overheads per machine hour.

Example

	Product A	Product B
Planned sales	100 units	200 units
Selling price	$40	$30
Opening inventory	12 units	20 units
Labour hours per unit	2 hours	1 hour
Machine hours per unit	1 hour	3 hours

Materials required:

	Material X	**Material Y**
Opening inventory of raw materials	36kg	44kg
Requirement per unit of product A	2kg	3kg
Requirement per unit of product B	2kg	1kg
Purchase price per kg	$0.50	$1.00

The company plans to halve all inventory levels over the period.

Labour rate per hour = $10

Variable overhead rate = $1.50 per machine hour

Fixed overhead rate = $0.50 per machine hour

Sales budget (principal budget factor)		Product A	Product B	Total
	Sales units	**100**	**200**	300 units
	Sales revenue	100 × 40 = $4,000	200 × $30 = $6,000	$10,000

Production budget		Product A	Product B
	Sales (units)	100	200
	Closing inventory (units)	6	10
	Opening inventory (units)	(12)	(20)
	Budgeted production (units)	**94**	**190**

Material budgets	Usage budget		Material X (kg)	Material Y (kg)
		Required for product A	94 × 2 = 188	94 × 3 = 282
		Required for product B	190 × 2 = 380	190 × 1 = 190
		Total	**568**	**472**
	Purchases budget		Material X	Material Y
		Usage budget (kg)	568	472
	Purchases budget		Material X	Material Y
		Usage budget (kg)	568	472
		Closing inventory (units)	18	22
		Opening inventory (units)	(36)	(44)
		Materials purchases budget (units)		
			550	450
		Materials purchases budget ($)	**$275**	**$450**
		Total materials purchases budget = $450 + $275 = $725		

Labour budget	Hours required for product A	94 × 2 = 188 hours
	Hours required for product B	190 × 1 = 190 hours
	Total hours required	378 hours
	Total labour budget	**$3,780**
Overhead budget	Machine hrs required for product A	94 × 1 = 94 hours
	Machine hrs required for product B	190 × 3 = 570 hours
	Total machine hours required	**664** hours
	Variable overhead budget	664 × 1.50 = $996
	Fixed overhead budget	664 × 0.50 = $332
	Total overhead budget	**$1,328**

Cash budgets

A **cash forecast** is an estimate of cash receipts and payments for a future period under existing conditions.

A **cash budget** is a commitment to a plan for cash receipts and payments for a future period after taking any action necessary to bring the forecast into line with the overall business plan.

Cash forecasts and budgets consider cash flows – so be careful to make sure that the transactions you are calculating involve **only cash items**.

Proforma for a cash budget

	July £	Aug £	Sept £
RECEIPTS			
Cash sales			
Cash from receivables			
Capital introduced			
Total receipts			
PAYMENTS			
Expenses			
Payments to payables			
Purchases of non-current assets			
Total payments			
Net cash flow			
Opening bank balance			
Closing bank balance			

Example of cash receipts from receivables

The forecast sales for an organisation are as follows:

Sales	January	February	March	April
	$	$	$	$
Sales	6,000	8,000	4,000	5,000

All sales are on credit and receivables tend to pay in the following pattern:

	%
In month of sale	10
In month after sale	40
Two months after sale	45

The organisation expects the rate of irrecoverable debts to be 5%.

Calculate the forecast cash receipts from receivables in April

Cash from:	$
April sales: 10% × $5,000	500
March sales: 40% × $4,000	1,600
February sales: 45% × $8,000	3,600
	5,700

Example of cash payment to payables

A manufacturing business makes and sells widgets. Each widget requires two units of raw materials, which cost $3 each. The business will take one month's credit.

Production quantities of widgets each month are as follows:

Month	Units
December	50,000
January	55,000
February	60,000
March	65,000

Calculate the payment to be made in April.

Quantity of raw material purchased:

	Production Units	Material (@ 2 units per widget) December Units	January Units	February Units	March Units
December	50,000	100,000			
January	55,000		110,000		
February	60,000			120,000	
March	65,000				130,000
		————	————	————	————
Total purchases		100,000	110,000	120,000	130,000
		————	————	————	————
At $3 per unit		300,000	330,000	360,000	390,000
			January $	February $	March $
Payment to suppliers			300,000	330,000	360,000

At the end of March, there will be payables of $390,000 for raw materials purchased, which will be paid in April.

What if analysis

'What if' analysis is a form of sensitivity analysis that allows:

- the effects of changes in one or more data value to be quickly recalculated
- budgets to be amended/adjusted easily.

Spreadsheets are very useful in what if analysis.

Scenario planning

Scenario planning has proved a very useful tool in forecasting, strategic planning and business modelling.

Budgetary control cycle

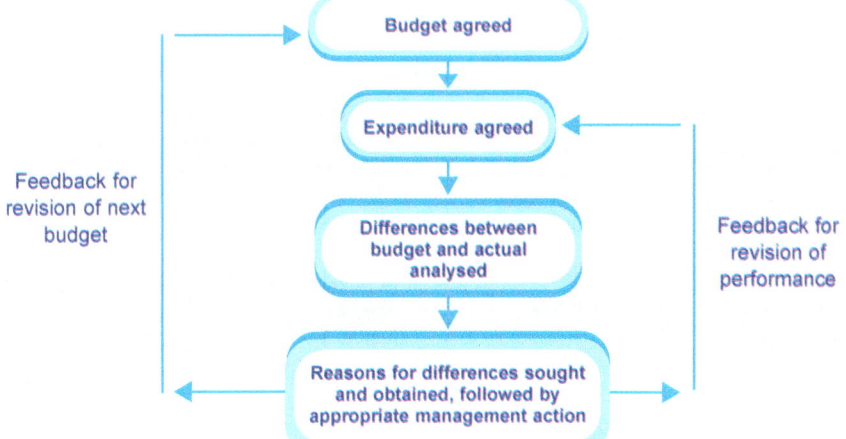

Feedback is the comparison of budget and actual performance with a view to revising plans, budgets or operations. The control action takes place after the event.

Planning is a form of **feedforward** control.

Fixed, flexible and flexed budgets

Fixed, flexible and flexed budgets are used within the budgetary control cycle where the planned budget is compared with the actual results.

Definition

Variances are differences arising between the original budget and actual results.

Adverse variances (Adv, A) decrease profits.

Favourable variances (Fav, F) increase profits.

Definition

A **fixed budget** is a budget produced for a single level of activity.

Fixed budgets:

* remain unchanged even though the volume of activity changes

* therefore, do not compare like with like

* therefore, do not assist in identifying the cause of variances.

Definition

A **flexible budget** is one which, by recognising cost behaviours patterns, is designed to change as volume of activity changes.

Definition

A **flexed budget** is the relevant section of the flexible budget that corresponds to the actual level of activity.

To produce a flexible and flexed budget:

* it is necessary to identify the cost behaviour of the different items in the original budget

* it may be necessary to use the high/low method to separate the fixed and variable elements of semi-variable costs.

Flexed budgets and budget variances

The overall differences between the original budget and actual results are total budget variances.

The total variance can be analysed into volume and expenditure variances:

- volume variance: shows the difference in costs due to the change in actual activity from budget. It is the difference between the fixed (original) and flexed budget

- expenditure variance: shows the difference in costs due to the actual expenditure differing from the fixed budget figures. It is the difference between the flexed budget and the actual results.

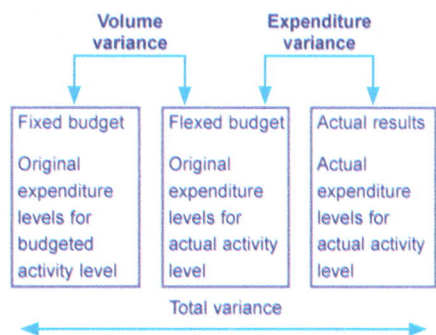

Example

	Fixed budget	Volume variance	Flexed budget	Expenditure variance	Actual results	Total variance
Production (units)	1000	200	800		800	
	$	$	$	$	$	$
Direct materials	500	100 (F)	400	(125) (A)	525	(25) (A)
Direct labour	2000	400 (F)	1600	250 (F)	1350	650 (F)
Variable production overhead	1000	200 (F)	800	(75) (A)	875	125 (F)
Fixed production overhead	400		400	(25) (A)	425	(25) (A)
Total	3900	700 (F)	3200	25 (F)	3175	725 (F)

Note: To convert from fixed budget to flexed budget, all estimates of variable cost expenditure are flexed with respect to output (800/1000). Fixed costs are not flexed with respect to output because they are fixed and do not depend on output volumes.

Responsibility accounting

Budgetary control and responsibility accounting are seen to be inseparable.

It is important to ensure that each manager has a well defined area of responsibility and the authority to make decisions within that area, and that no parts of the organisation remain as 'grey' areas where it is uncertain who is responsible for them. If this is put into effect properly, each area of the organisation's activities is the responsibility of a manager. This structure should then be reflected in the organisation chart.

An area of responsibility may be structured as:

- a cost centre – where the manager is responsible for cost control only
- a revenue centre – where the manager is responsible for generation of revenues only
- a profit centre – the manager has control over sales revenues as well as costs
- an investment centre – the manager is empowered to take decisions about capital investment for his department.

Each centre has its own budget, and the manager receives control information relevant to that budget centre. Costs (and possibly revenue, assets and liabilities) must be traced to the person primarily responsible for taking the related decisions, and identified with the appropriate department.

Controllable and uncontrollable costs

Controllable costs and revenues are those costs and revenues which result from decisions within the authority of a particular manager or unit within the organisation. These should be used to assess the performance of managers.

The aim under a responsibility accounting system will be to assign and report on the cost to the person having primary responsibility.

Investment appraisal

In this chapter

- Types of interest.
- Payback period.
- Net present value.
- Internal rate of return (IRR).
- Annuities.
- Perpetuities.

This chapter contains 3 main techniques for appraisal of investments – payback period, net present value and internal rate of return. You need to know the calculations and the theory behind each technique.

Types of interest

Simple interest is calculated based on the original sum invested. Any interest earned in earlier periods is not included. Simple interest is often used for a single investment period that is less than a year.

Compound interest calculates the future (or terminal value) of a given sum invested today for a number of years.

The **nominal interest rate** is the stated interest rate for a time period – for example a month or a year.

The **effective interest rate** is the interest rate that includes the effects of compounding a nominal interest rate.

Payback period

The payback period is the time a project will take to pay back the money spent on it. It is based on expected cash flows and provides a measure of liquidity. This is the time which elapses until the initial investment is recovered. It considers cash flows only. It can be calculated with and without discounted cash flows.

- Compare the payback period to the company's maximum return time allowed and if the payback is quicker the project should be accepted.

- Faced with mutually exclusive projects choose the project with the quickest payback.

	Payback Period	
Year	Cash flow $000	Cumulative cash flow $000
0	(450)	(450)
1	200	(250)
2	150	(100)
3	50	(50)
4	100	50
5	120	

Payback period = 3 years and 50/100 × 12 months

= 3 years and 6 months

	Discounted Payback period			
Year	Cash flow $000	Discount factor	Discounted cash flow $000	Cumulative discounted cash flow
0	(450)		(450)	(450)
1	200	0.909	182	(268)
2	150	0.826	124	(144)
3	50	0.751	38	(106)
4	100	0.683	68	(38)
5	120	0.621	75	37
Discounted payback period = 4 years and 38/75 × 12 months				
= 4 years and 6 months				

Advantages	Disadvantages
• Simple to understand	• Is not a measure of absolute profitability
• A project with a long payback period tends to be riskier than one with a short payback period.	• Ignores the time value of money Note: A discounted payback period may be calculated to overcome this problem
• Payback is a simple measure of Risk	• Does not take into account cash flows beyond the payback period
• Uses cash flows, not subjective accounting profits	
• Emphasises the cash flows in the earlier years	
• Firms selecting projects on the basis of payback periods may avoid liquidity problems	

Net present value

The NPV represents the surplus funds (after funding the investment) earned on the project. This means that it tells us the impact on shareholder wealth. The net benefit or loss of benefit in present value terms from an investment opportunity.

- Any project with a positive NPV is viable.
- Projects with a negative NPV are not viable.
- Faced with mutually exclusive projects, choose the project with the highest NPV.

Example

Mickey Ltd is considering two mutually exclusive projects with the following details:

Project A

Initial investment $450,000

Scrap value in year 5 $20,000

Year:	1	2	3	4	5
Annual cash flows ($000)	200	150	100	100	100

Project B

Initial investment $100,000
Scrap value in year 5 $10,000

Year:	1	2	3	4	5
Annual cash flows ($000)	50	40	30	20	20

Assume that the initial investment is at the start of the project and the annual cash flows are at the end of each year.

Required:

Calculate the Net Present Value for Projects A and B if the relevant cost of capital is 10%. Calculate which project has the highest NPV.

Year	Discount factor	Project A Cash flow $000	Present value $000	Project B Cash flow $000	Present value $000
0		(450)	(450)	(100)	(100)
1	0.909	200	181.8	50	45.45
2	0.826	150	123.9	40	33.04
3	0.751	100	75.1	30	22.53
4	0.683	100	68.3	20	13.66
5	0.621	120	74.52	30	18.63
		NPV	= 73.62	NPV	= 33.31

Advantages	Disadvantages
• Does consider the time value of money	• Fairly complex
• It is a measure of absolute Profitability	• Not well understood by nonfinancial managers
• Considers cash flows	• It may be difficult to determine the cost of capital
• It considers the whole life of the Project	
• A company selecting projects on the basis of NPV maximisation should maximise shareholders	

Internal rate of return (IRR)

This is the rate of return, or discount rate, at which the project has a NPV of zero.

- If the IRR is greater than the cost of capital the project should be accepted.
- Faced with mutually exclusive projects choose the project with the higher IRR.

Technique:

(1) Calculate two NPVs for the project at two different costs of capital

(2) Use the following formula to find the IRR:

$$IRR = L + \frac{NL}{NL - NH} \times (H - L)$$

where:

L = Lower rate of interest

H = Higher rate of interest

NL = NPV at lower rate of interest

NH = NPV at higher rate of interest

Example

Calculate the internal rate of return.

At 20% the NPV is $8,510

At 30% the NPV is − $9,150

$$IRR = 20 + \frac{8,510}{8,510 - -9,150} \times (30 - 20)$$

IRR = 24.8%

Advantages	Disadvantages
• Does consider the time value of money • As a percentage return it is easily understood by nonfinancial managers • Considers cash flows • It considers the whole life of the project • It can be calculated without reference to the cost of capital • A company selecting projects where the IRR exceeds the cost of capital should increase shareholders' wealth	• It is not a measure of absolute profitability • Interpolation only provides an estimate of the true IRR • Fairly complicated to calculate – although spreadsheets now have built in programs • The IRR of projects may conflict with the NPV. If this occurs the NPV must take precedence

Annuities

An annuity is a constant annual cash flow for a number of years.

The formula is:

$$AF = \frac{1 - (1+r)^{-n}}{r}$$

Perpetuities

A perpetuity is an annual cash flow that occurs forever.

The formula is:

$$PV = \frac{\text{Cash flow}}{r}$$

or

$$PV = \text{cash flow} \times \frac{1}{r}$$

Standard costing

In this chapter

- The purpose of standard costing.
- Advantages and disadvantages of standard costing.
- Types of standard.
- Variance calculations.
- The causes of variances.
- Operating statements.

This is a very popular topic for multiple-choice questions! Learn the techniques so you can calculate the variances quickly and accurately.

Don't rely on common sense with fixed overhead variances under absorption costing – learn it!

One way that the examiner can easily test your understanding of variances is to ask you to calculate the following instead of straightforward variance calculations:

- actual figures from variances and standards

- standards from variances and actual figures.

The purpose of standard costing

Standard costing helps management control the business:

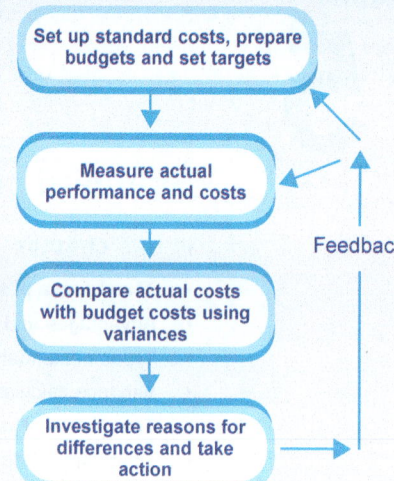

Standard costs are normally collected on a standard cost card.

- They may be based on absorption costing or marginal costing (variable cost only).

Advantages and disadvantages of standard costing

Advantages	Disadvantages
• Detailed examination of the organisation when standards are being set	• Standards can quickly become out of date
• Comparison of actual cost to standard cost for performance evaluation	• Establishing standards, monitoring the system and investigating variances is costly
• Facilitates management by exception by concentrating on investigation of most significant variances	• Unrealistic standards can demotivate staff
• Simplifies bookkeeping and inventory records where all inventory is valued at standard	

Types of standard

Ideal	Attainable
What would be expected under perfect operating conditions	What would be expected under normal operating conditions
Basic	**Current**
A standard left unchanged from period to period	A standard adjusted for specific issues relating to the current period

Variance calculations

Points to remember

There are two areas where the variance calculations depends on whether you are working with a marginal or an absorption costing systems:

- the sales volume variance
- fixed overhead variances.

	Marginal costing	Absorption costing
Sales volume variance	• Calculated using the standard contribution per unit	• Calculated using the standard profit per unit
	Note – The standard selling price is not used because when volumes change so do production costs and the purpose of the variance is to show the impact on profit or contribution.	

	Marginal costing	Absorption costing
Fixed overhead variances	• Marginal costing does not relate fixed overheads to cost units.	• Fixed overheads are related to cost units by using absorption rates.
	• There is no under- or over-absorption, and the fixed overhead incurred is as shown in the statement of profit or loss as a period cost.	• The fixed overhead total variance is equivalent to the under- or over-absorption of overhead in a period.
	• There is therefore no fixed overhead volume variance.	• The fixed overhead volume variance can be further subdivided into capacity and efficiency variance.
	The fixed overhead expenditure variance is the difference between actual expenditure and budgeted expenditure and is the total variance.	

Calculating variances

SALES VARIANCES

Sales volume variance

Absorption costing

(Budgeted quantity sold – actual quantity sold) × standard profit per unit

Marginal costing

(Budgeted quantity sold – actual quantity sold) × standard contribution per unit

Sales price variance

(Budgeted sales price – actual sales price) × actual quantity sold

Example

JDC operates a standard cost accounting system. The following information has been extracted from its standard cost card and budgets:

Budgeted sales volume	5,000 units
Budgeted selling price	$10.00 per unit
Standard variable cost	$5.60 per unit
Standard total cost	$7.50 per unit

JDC's actual sales were 4,500 units at a selling price of $12.00. What is the sales volume variance and the sales price variance under marginal and absorption costing?

Solution

Standard contribution/unit = $10 – $5.60 = $4.40

Sales volume variance under marginal costing = (Actual sales – Budgeted sales) × Standard contribution per unit = $(4,500 – 5,000) × $4.40 = $2,200 (A)

Standard profit/unit = $10 – $7.50 = $2.50

Sales volume variance under absorption costing = (actual sales – Budgeted sales) × Standard profit per unit = (4,500 - 5,000) × $2.50 = $1,250 (A)

Sales price variance under marginal and absorption costing = (Actual sales price – budgeted sales prices) × Actual quantity = ($12 – $10) × 4,500 = $9,000 (F)

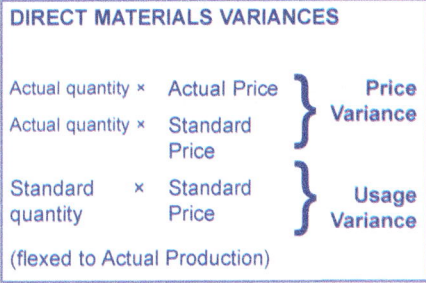

DIRECT MATERIALS VARIANCES

Actual quantity ×	Actual Price	Price Variance
Actual quantity ×	Standard Price	
Standard quantity ×	Standard Price	Usage Variance

(flexed to Actual Production)

Example

Company A uses 6kg of Material M in its unique product P. Each kg of M costs £5. In January, 6,500kg of M were used to produce 1,000 units of P, at a cost of £39,000.

Calculate :

(i) the material price variance,
(ii) the material usage variance.

Solution

(i)

Actual Quantity	×	Actual Price		
6,500 kgs	×	£6.00	=	£39,000

Actual Quantity	×	Standard Price		
6,500 kgs	×	£5.00	=	£32,500

Material price variance   =   £6,500 A

The price variance is adverse for Material M, the standard material cost was lower than actual material costs.

(ii)

Actual Quantity × Standard Price
  6,500 kgs   × £5.00 = £32,500

Standard Quantity × Standard Price
  6,000 kgs   × £5.00 = £30,000

Material usage variance = £2,500 A

The usage variance is adverse, so actual materials used were more than the standard quantity.

DIRECT LABOUR VARIANCES

Actual hours ×	Actual Rate	**Rate Variance**
Actual hours ×	Standard Rate	
Standard × hours	Standard Rate	**Efficiency Variance**

(flexed to Actual Production)

Example

The standard direct labour cost of Product H is $21 per unit, and each unit is expected to take 3.5 hours to make. The budget was to produce 22,000 units, but in the period, only 21,000 units were actually made. The time required to produce these units was 75,000 hours, which had a labour cost of $431,250. What was the direct labour rate variance and the direct labour efficiency variance in the period?

Solution

Actual hours × Actual rate = $431,250
75,000

                         Rate variance = $18,750 (F)

Actual hours × Standard rate = $450,000
75,000 $21/3.50

                         Efficiency variance = $9,000 (A)

Standard hours × Standard rate = $441,000
21,000 × 3.5 $21/3.50

VARIABLE OVERHEADS VARIANCES

Actual hours ×	Actual Rate	} Expenditure Variance
Actual hours ×	Standard Rate	
Standard hours ×	Standard Rate	} Efficiency Variance

(flexed to Actual Production)

FIXED OVERHEADS VARIANCES

Absorption costing

Actual expenditure

Expenditure variance

Budgeted expenditure

Volume variance

Actual units produced × fixed overhead absorption rate per unit

or, splitting down the volume variance into capacity and efficiency variances:

Actual expenditure

Expenditure variance

Budgeted expenditure

Capacity variance

Actual hours × fixed overhead absorption rate per hour

Efficiency variance

Standard hours for actual production × fixed overhead absorption rate per hour

Example

A company operates a standard absorption costing system. The standard fixed production overhead rate is $15 per hour.

The following data relate to last month :

Actual hours worked	5,500
Budgeted hours	5,000
Standard hours for actual production	4,800

Calculate :

(i) the fixed production overhead capacity variance

(ii) the fixed production overhead efficiency variance

Solution

(i) Capacity variance (5,000 – 5,500) hours at $15 per hour = $7,500 F

Note that working more hours than budgeted produces a favourable fixed overhead capacity variance.

This is because working more hours does not cause more fixed overhead expenditure, but does make better use of the fixed resources.

(ii) Efficiency variance

Standard hours for actual production 4,800 × OAR $15	=	$72,000
Less Actual hours 5,500 × OAR $15	=	$82,500
Efficiency variance	=	$10,500 A

The causes of variances

Variance	Possible causes
Sales volume variance	• Price change
	• Change in size of market
	• Change in market share – competition
Sales price variance	• Deliberate – e.g. drop price to boost sales
	• Due to change in quality?
	• Competition
Materials price variance	• Change in supplier
	• Different material bought
	• Efforts of purchasing department
	• Commodity price changes
Materials usage variance	• Different materials (link to price?)
	• Different machinery
	• Efforts of production department
	• Change in mix of materials?

Labour price (or rate) variance	• Productivity link
	• Strikes
	• Different grade of labour
Labour efficiency variance	• Link to rate?
	• Change in quality of materials
	• Change in machinery
	• Efforts of production department
Variable O/H expenditure (or rate) variance	• Machines wearing out?
	• Machines overworked due to increase in production volume
Variable O/H efficiency variance	• Same as for labour efficiency variance
Fixed O/H expenditure variance	• Change in rent, etc.

Operating statements

Variances are summarised in an operating statement. The main differences between absorption and marginal costing operating statements are as follows:

- the marginal costing operating statement has a sales volume variance that is calculated using the standard contribution per unit (rather than a standard profit per unit as in absorption costing)

- there is no fixed overhead volume variance in a marginal costing system.

Operating statements – total absorption costing

Variances are often summarised in an operating statement (or reconciliation statement).

Absorption costing operating statement			$
Budgeted profit			
Sales volume variance (using profit per unit)			___
Standard profit on actual sales			
Sales price variance			
Cost variances:	F	A	
	$	$	
Material price			
Material usage			
Labour rate			
Labour efficiency			
Variable overhead rate			
Variable overhead efficiency			
Fixed overhead volume – Production			
Fixed overhead expenditure – Production			
Fixed overhead expenditure – Non-Production	___	___	
Total			___
Actual profit			___
(Note the bold highlights the differences from the marginal costing version.)			

Marginal costing operating statement			$
Budgeted contribution			
Sales volume variance (using contribution per unit)			____
Standard contribution on actual sales			
Sales price variance			____
Cost variances:			
	F	A	
	$	$	
Material price			
Material usage			
Labour rate			
Labour efficiency			
Variable overhead rate			
Variable overhead efficiency			
Actual contribution			
Budgeted fixed on			
Fixed overhead expenditure – Production			
Fixed overhead expenditure – Non-Production	____	____	
Total			____
Actual profit			____

Note

There is no fixed overhead volume variance (and therefore capacity and efficiency variances) in a marginal costing operating statement.

16

Performance measurement techniques

In this chapter

- Financial performance measurement.
- Divisional performance.
- Non-financial performance measurement.
- The Balanced Scorecard.
- Benchmarking.
- Non-profit and public sector.
- Cost control and cost reduction.

This chapter contains the formulae for the performance indicators that you are likely to come across.

You need to make sure you use the right ones in the right situations so make sure you read the scenarios/questions carefully.

Financial performance measurement

Profitability

Return on capital employed (ROCE) = operating profit ÷ (noncurrent liabilities + total equity) %

Return on sales (ROS) = operating profit ÷ revenue %

Gross margin = gross profit ÷ revenue %

Asset turnover = revenue ÷ capital employed

Liquidity

Current ratio = current assets ÷ current liabilities

Quick ratio = (current assets – inventory) ÷ current liabilities

Activity

Inventory days = inventory ÷ cost of sales × 365

Receivable days = receivables ÷ credit sales × 365

Payable days = payables ÷ credit purchases × 365

Risk

Capital gearing = noncurrent liabilities (debt) ÷ ordinary shareholders funds (equity) %

or

Capital gearing = noncurrent liabilities (debt) ÷ (noncurrent liabilities + ordinary shareholders funds (debt + equity)) %

Interest cover = operating profit ÷ finance cost.

Divisional Performance

Measurement of divisional performance needs to be based on controllable costs and controllable revenue therefore controllable profits.

Two calculations that can be used to measure divisional performance are return on investment and residual income.

$$ROI = \frac{\text{Controllable profit}}{\text{Controllable capital employed}} \times 100$$

RI = Controllable profit – Notional interest on capital

Non-financial performance measurement

Examples of non-financial indicators:

- Competitiveness
- Resource utilisation
- Quality of service
- Customer satisfaction
- Quality of working
- Innovation
- Responsiveness (lead time)
- Quality of output
- Flexibility (ability to react to changing demand and a changing environment)

Productivity measures

Production/volume ratio

$$\frac{\text{Actual output measured in standard hours}}{\text{Budgeted production hours}} \times 100$$

Capacity ratio

$$\frac{\text{Actual production hours worked}}{\text{Budgeted production hours}} \times 100$$

Efficiency ratio

$$\frac{\text{Actual output measured in standard hours}}{\text{Actual production hours worked}} \times 100$$

Measuring quality

Quality is seen to be a particularly important nonfinancial performance indicator in the service sector. Quality can be measured by:

* customer surveys
* management inspections
* fault monitoring.

Total Quality Management (TQM)

* Total – means that everyone in the value chain is involved in the process, including employees, customer and suppliers
* Quality – products and services must meet the customers' requirements
* Management – quality is actively managed rather than controlled so that problems are prevented from occurring.

TQM Priniples

* **Get it right, first time**
  Costs of prevention are less than the costs of correction; achieve zero rejects and 100% quality

* **Continuous improvement**
  A zero defect goal may not be obtainable. It does however provide a target

* **Customer focus**
  Quality is examined from a customer perspective, aimed at meeting customer needs and expectations.

Conformance costs:	Non-conformance costs:
Appraisal costs	Internal failure costs
Prevention costs	External failure costs

The Balanced Scorecard

BALANCED SCORECARD STRATEGIC PERSPECTIVES

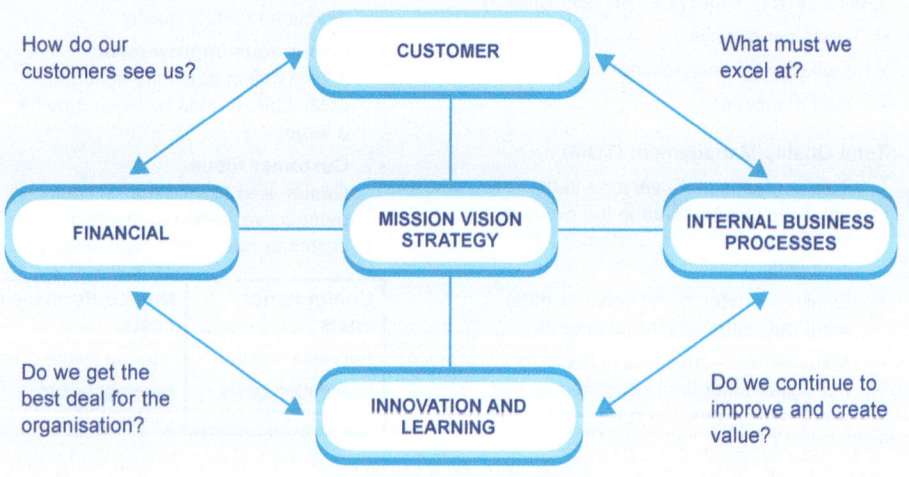

How do our customers see us?

What must we excel at?

Do we get the best deal for the organisation?

Do we continue to improve and create value?

Advantages	Disadvantages
• uses four perspectives less able to distort the performance measure	• large numbers of calculations required
• harder to hide bad performance	• subjective
• long term rather than short term	• comparison with other businesses is not easy
• focuses on KPIs	• arbitrary nature of arriving at the overall index of performance
• KPIs can be changed as the business changes	

Benchmarking

Benchmarking is the management process which involves comparison of competences with best practice including comparison beyond the organisation's own industry. There are several types of benchmarking including:

- Internal benchmarks – comparisons between different departments or functions within an organisation.

- Competitive benchmarks – comparisons with competitors in the business sector – through inter-firm comparison schemes.

- Functional benchmarks – comparisons with organisations with similar core activities that are not a competitor.

- Strategic benchmarks – comparisons of market share and profit margins.

Non-profit and public sector

There are said to be two main problems involved in assessing performance of these organisations:

- the problem of identifying and measuring objectives

- the problem of identifying and measuring outputs.

Value for money (VFM)

VFM concept revolves around the 3Es, as follows:

- Economy (an input measure) – measures the relationship between money spent and the inputs. Are the resources used the cheapest possible for the quality required?

$$\frac{\text{Standard input}}{\text{Actual input}} \times 100$$

- Efficiency (link inputs with outputs) – is the maximum output being achieved from the resources used?

$$\frac{\text{Actual output}}{\text{Actual input}} \times 100$$

- Effectiveness (links outputs with objectives) – to what extent to which the outputs generated achieve the objectives of the organisation

$$\frac{\text{Actual output}}{\text{Standard output}} \times 100$$

Cost control and cost reduction

Cost control – cost control involves the setting of targets for cost centre managers and then monitoring performance against those targets.

Cost reduction – cost reduction is the reduction in unit cost of goods or services without impairing suitability for the use intended i.e. without reducing value to the customer.

Value analysis – a systematic examination of factors affecting the cost of a product or service, in order to devise means of achieving the specified purpose most economically at the required standard of quality and reliability.

Value engineering – attempts to design the best possible value at the lowest possible cost into a new product. This cost can then be used in a target costing system.

Work study – a systematic examination of the methods of carrying out activities in order to improve the effective use of resources and to set up standards of performance for the activities carried out.

17

Presenting information

In this chapter

- Writing reports.
- Graphs and charts.

You will need to be able to interpret and do the relevant calculations for different types of graphs and charts.

Writing reports

Four stages:

1 Prepare

2 Plan

3 Write

4 Review

Structure:

- Title
- Introduction
- Analysis
- Conclusion
- Appendices

Graphs and charts

Graphical methods of presentation are often clearer to the user than written or numerical presentation.

Key benefits of data visualisation include:

- Accessibility – data visualisation graphics and dashboards are designed to be user friendly and intuitive.

- Real-time synchronising – real time data with data visualisation tools gives live up-to-date numbers in a clear, informative style.

- Performance optimisation – the immediacy and clarity of the information being displayed supports better decision-making.

- Insight and understanding – combining data and visualising it in a new way can lead to improved understanding and fresh insights.

Simple bar chart

Production
(m tonnes)

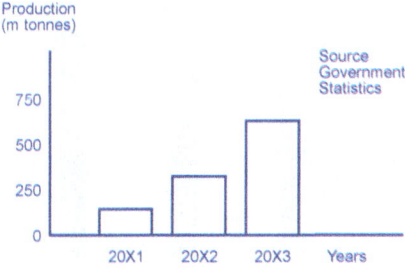

A simple bar chart is where one variable only is being illustrated.

Component bar chart

Production
(m tonnes)

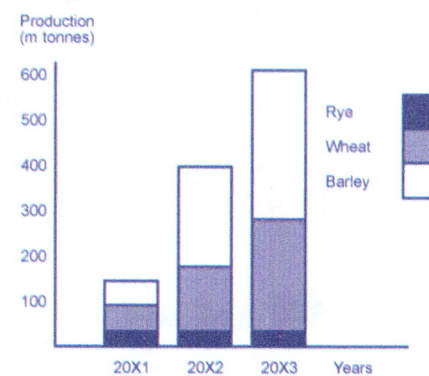

A component bar chart is used when each total figure in the data is made up of a number of different components and it is important that these component elements are shown as well as the total figure.

Percentage component bar chart

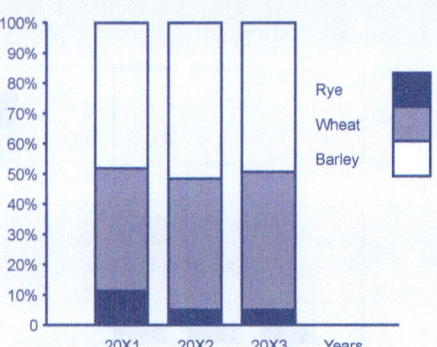

A percentage component bar chart is one where the actual values of each component are not shown but the percentage of the total for each component is. The bars in this type of chart are all the same height (representing 100%) and are split according to the proportions of each component element.

Compound bar chart

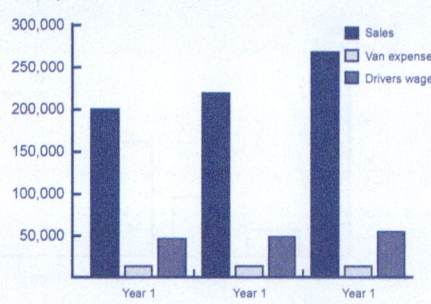

Compound bar charts are sometimes termed multiple bar charts. A compound bar chart is one where there is more than one bar for each subdivision of the chart.

It is a suitable format if the total of each component of the bar chart has no significance.

Multiple line chart

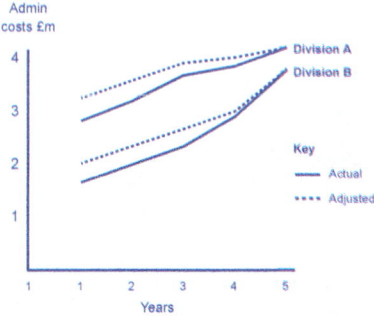

In many instances it will be found that data can be more clearly and understandably presented in the form of a line graph, especially if we are consider the change in an item over time.

Pie chart

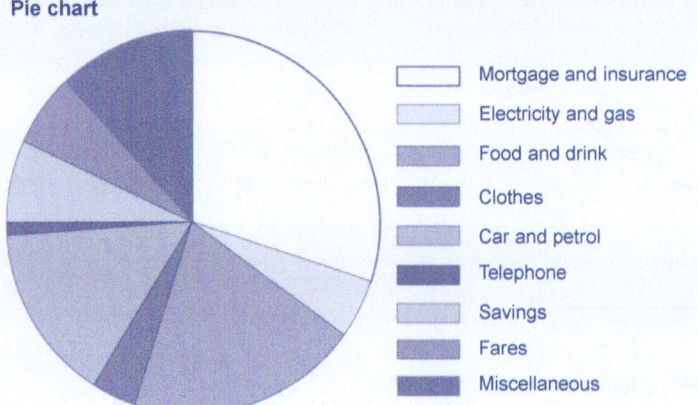

- Mortgage and insurance
- Electricity and gas
- Food and drink
- Clothes
- Car and petrol
- Telephone
- Savings
- Fares
- Miscellaneous

Constructing a pie chart

- Calculate the total value of all components of the numerical data
- Convert each component of data into 'degrees' of the circle:
  360°/Total value of the data = number of degrees per unit
- Calculate the size of the wedge required to represent each element of the data.

18

Spreadsheets

In this chapter

- Spreadsheets.
- Uses of spreadsheets.

You could be asked why spreadsheets are useful to a business. Equally you could be asked to combine your knowledge of spreadsheets with calculations in earlier chapters to produce formulae.

Spreadsheets

A spreadsheet is a computer package that is used to manipulate data.

To enter a formula

- select the cell where you want to enter the formula

- press the equal sign (=) on the keyboard (or click on the sign in the formula bar, if one is shown)

- key in the formula directly from the keyboard or use the mouse to select the cells you want in the formula. There are no spaces in a formula

- press the <Enter> key

- when you have entered a formula, the resulting value appears in that cell. The formula is only visible in the formula bar.

Uses of spreadsheets

Much of the data of a company is likely to be held on a number of spreadsheets. They are a convenient way of setting up all sorts of charts, records and tables, including:

Budgeting and forecasting

Preparing budgets and forecasts are classic applications of spreadsheets, as they allow estimates to be changed without having to recalculate everything manually.

'What-if' analysis

- The power of spreadsheets is that the data held in any one cell can be made dependent on that held in other cells.

- This means that changing a value in one cell can set off a chain reaction of changes through other related cells.

- This allows 'what if?' analysis to be quickly and easily carried out, e.g. 'what if sales are 10% lower than expected?'

Reporting performance

Performance appraisal usually involves calculating ratios, possibly involving comparatives between companies and from one year to the next.

- A neat way of doing this is to input the raw data, such as financial statements on one sheet and calculate the ratios on another.

Variance analysis

Variance analysis involves management comparing actual results with budget and then investigating the differences.

Advantages of spreadsheets

Spreadsheets are designed to analyse data and sort list items, not for long term storage of raw data. A spreadsheet should be used for 'crunching' numbers and storage of single list items. Advantages of spreadsheets include the following:

- Spreadsheet programs are relatively easy to use.
- Little training is required to get started with using spreadsheets.
- Most data managers are familiar with spreadsheets.
- They also include graphing functions that allow for quick reporting and analysis of data. There is more on the graphics function of spreadsheets at the end of this section.

Disadvantages of spreadsheets

Disadvantages of spreadsheets include the following:

- Data must be recopied over and over again to maintain it in separate data files.

- Spreadsheets are not able to identify data errors efficiently.

- Spreadsheets lack detailed sorting and querying abilities.

- There can be sharing violations among users wishing to view or change data at the same time.

- Spreadsheets are restricted to a finite number of records, and can require a large amount of hard drive space for data storage.

Index

M

N

O

Z